WHAT BECOMES OF THE SOUL AFTER DEATH

Owing to the antiquity and rarity of this book, certain pages are regrettably absent, and readability is compromised due to the blurring of the original text. If you possess any insights regarding the availability of these missing sections, kindly inform us. Your assistance is crucial in ensuring the completion of this significant work for the benefit of future generations.

WHAT BECOMES OF THE SOUL AFTER DEATH

SWAMI SIVANANDA SARSWATI

GYAN

Published by

Gyan Publishing House
5, Ansari Road
Daryaganj, New Delhi-110002
Phone: 011-47034999, 9811692060
E-mail: books@gyanbooks.com

Distribution Network
gyanbooks.com
India, USA, Canada, UK, Australia

ISBN: 978-93-7316-154-9 (HB)

First Published, 1967

2nd Impression 2026

Printed at: Gyan Press, Delhi.

WHAT BECOMES OF THE SOUL AFTER DEATH
Author: SWAMI SIVANANDA SARSWATI

WHAT BECOMES OF THE SOUL AFTER DEATH

(REVISED AND ENLARGED)

By

SRI SWAMI SIVANANDA

Published By

THE DIVINE LIFE SOCIETY

P O SIVANANDANAGAR,

Dt Tehri-Garhwal, U P, Himalayas, India

1967

OM

DEDICATED

To

LORD YAMA, MARKANDEYA, NACHIKETAS SAVITRI AND NANDI, THE ETERNAL ATTENDANT OF LORD SIVA, WHO HAVE ALL UNRAVELLED THE MYSTERIES OF THE LIFE BEYOND DEATH

OM

5th December, 1957

Children of Immortality!

There is a living, unchanging, eternal Consciousness that underlies all names and forms. That is God or Brahman.

God is the end of all actions. He is the end of all Sadhanas, Yoga practices. Seek Him. Realise Him. Only then can you be free and perfect. Look upon the world as a mirage. Lead a life of selfless service, renunciation, dispassion, prayer and meditation. You will soon attain God-realisation.

May God bless you. Om Tat Sat.

Thy own Atman,

HIS HOLINESS SRI SWAMI SIVANANDAJI

PUBLISHERS' NOTE

The problem of life beyond death has ever been a most fascinating one from time immemorial Man has always been intrigued by the question, "What becomes of the Soul after Death?" The present volume, as the title suggests, treats in detail of the subject and furnishes an answer to the agelong question

In recent times there has been much speculation on this problem. This has led to a lot of research work too The fact of continuity of consciousness after physical death has come to be accepted as such by most of the modern thinkers, latest of whom, the famous scientist, Dr J B Rhine, has expressed himself in favour of such belief Many books have been written on this subject, but hitherto most of the works deal mainly with the astral or other spirit world It has mostly been the study of the conditions in the Pretaloka which is merely one among the numerous supramundane planes beyond the grave Spiritism, seance and the testimony of recognised mediums have for most part featured prominently in all such works

This present book by Sri Swami Sivanandaji is a departure from the usual line in that it is based, to a great extent, upon authoritative scriptural texts and upon knowledge derived through reasoning, deep reflection and personal meditation It throws a flood of light upon all aspects of post-mortem existence not adequately dealt with in other works The book also gives valuable information about the different beliefs on this subject, of the various races and religions

The portions giving the inner meaning and the esoteric significance of the different practices and customs in connection with the dead form a most informative one The appendix and the stories in the end and the very interesting poems in the beginning are most thought-provoking and highly inspiring

We feel that the perusal of the present work will confirm man s belief that 'death is not the end of life', that his actions here unfailingly react upon him in the 'after state too and will stimulate his Vichara We have no doubt that the reader will be helped to make a proper evaluation of the real worth of this physical existence upon the earth plane in the light of this new knowledge of the supracorporeal states of being

—*The Publishers*

INTRODUCTION

Paraloka-Vidya or the science about the departed souls and their planes of living is a subject of absorbing interest It is a mysterious Science which contains many secrets or hidden wonders It has intimate connection with Panchagni Vidya of the Chhandogya Upanishad The doctrine of reincarnation or metempsychosis, transmigration of the souls and spiritualism come under the Paraloka Vidya Everybody is curious and anxious to know this science

Great scientists, the inventors of many marvellous things, mighty Emperors who have done stupendous works, inspired poets, wonderful artists, many Brahmins, Rishis, Yogis have come and gone You are all extremely anxious to know what has become of them Do they still exist? What is there at the other side of death? Have they become nonexistent or have they dwindled into an airy nothing? Such questions do arise spontaneously in the hearts of all The same question arises today as it arose thousands of years ago No one can stop it, because it is inseparably connected with our nature

Death is a subject which is of the deepest interest to everyone One day or other all must die The terror of death overshadows the lives of all human beings It brings considerably unnecessary sorrow, suffering and anxiety to the survivors who are anxi ous to know about the fate of the departed souls

In the West also this question has aroused . great deal of interest and attention in certain scien tific circles. Much investigation has been made Bu the researchers have, however, been confined more o less to find out whether or not the individuality sur vives and persists after the dissolution of the phys cal body. This has been proved in the affirmative b actual communication with the spirit world throug science, mediumship etc

A knowledge of this science will rob death of a its terror and sorrow and enable you to see it in th proper light and to understand its place in the schem of your evolution. It will certainly goad you to fin out suitable methods to conquer death and attain im mortality It will forcibly urge you to take to th study of Brahma Vidya in right earnest and find ou the true Master or illumined sage who can put you the right path of Truth and explain to you the my teries of Kaivalya or Brahma Jnana

The other side of death is accurately describ in this book It has been scientifically examined an carefully described This book contains abundant i formation on this subject It will give you a weal of facts on this topic It contains the essence of t Upanishadic teachings

You have suffered very much simply out of ign rance and superstition concerning this most impo tant matter If you go through this book careful the veil of ignorance will be removed. You will freed from the horrors of death

The one aim of all Yoga Sadhanas is to face death fearlessly and joyfully. A Yogi or a Sage or even a real Aspirant has no fear of death Death is terribly afraid of those who do Japa, meditation and Kirtan He and his messengers dare not approach them Lord Krishna says in the Bhagavad Gita, "Having come to Me, these Mahatmas come not again to birth, the place of pain and non-eternity, they have gone to the highest bliss" Chap. VIII-15

Death is painful to a worldly man A desireless man never weeps when he dies A full-blown Jnani never dies His Prana never departs Your highest duty is to prepare for a peaceful life hereafter Conquer the fear of death Conquest of fear of death, conquest of death is the highest utility of all Spiritual Sadhana Pray to the Lord to enable you to worship Him in every birth of yours End the cycle of birth if you want everlasting bliss Live in the eternal Atman and be happy for ever

Bhishma had death at his command (Ichha Mrityu) Savitri brought back Satyavan, her husband, to life through her power of chastity. Markandeya conquered death through worship of Lord Siva You also can conquer death through devotion, knowledge and power of Brahmacharya

PRAYER OF A DYING MAN

(Isavasya Upanishad)

हिरण्मयेन पात्रेण सत्यस्यापिहित मुखम् ।
तत्त्व पूषन्नपावृणु सत्यधर्माय दृष्टये ॥

The face of Truth is covered by a golden vessel Remove, O Sun, the covering, for the law of the Truth, that I may behold It!

पूषन्नेकर्षे यम सूर्य प्राजापत्य व्यूह रश्मीन्समूह ।
तेजो यत्ते रूपं कल्याणतम तत्ते पश्यामि योसावसौ
पुरुष सोऽहमस्मि ॥

O Pushan (Sun nourisher), only seer (sole traveller of the heavens), controller of all (Yama), Surya, son of Prajapati disperse the rays and gather up thy burning light I behold thy glorious form I am He, the Purusha within thee!

वायुरनिलममृतमथेद भस्मान्त शरीरम् ।
ॐ क्रतो स्मर कृत स्मर क्रतो स्मर कृतं स्मर ॥

(Let my) Prana melt into the all-pervading Air, the eternal Sutratman, and let this body be burnt by fire to ashes OM! O mind! remember my deeds! O mind! remember, remember my deeds!

अग्ने नय सुपथा राये अस्मान् विश्वानि देव वयुनानि विद्वान् ।
युयोध्यस्मज्जुहुराणमेनो भूयिष्ठां ते नम उक्तिं विधेम ॥

O Agne' lead us on to wealth (bliss, Mukti, beatitude) by a good path, as Thou knowest, O God' all the ways Remove the crooked sin from within us. We offer Thee our best salutations'

ODE TO DEATH

O Death! O Lord Yama! Good-bye unto Thee
Thou art administering the laws of Ishwara
All fall a prey to Thee,
All come into Thy jaws,

Thou art time,
Thou art Dharma Raja,
O! Omniscient Kala (Time),
Thou art the dispenser of the Law

Thou art acquainted
With the three periods of time
Thou once initiated Nachiketas
Into the mysteries of Atman or Brahma Vidya

I have transcended Time and Death
I am Eternity
Where is Time in Eternity?
Time is a mental creation,

I have transcended mind,
I am not afraid of Death
I am beyond Thy reach now,
I bid Thee farewell now,

I am grateful for all Thy kind acts
Salutations unto Thee, O Lord Yama!
I wish to attain Videhamukti now,
I will merge in the Supreme Self

WHAT IS REAL LIFE ?

To live in the eternal Atman,
To taste the bliss of the soul
To worship the Lord at all times,
Is real Life

To do Japa of Lord's name,
To sing His glory constantly,
To remember Him at all times,
Is real Life

To practise Yama, Niyama,
To serve the poor and the sick,
To hear the Srutis
Is real Life

To reflect and meditate,
To serve the Guru,
To follow his instructions,
Is real Life

To realise one's own self,
To behold the one self everywhere,
To attain Brahma Jnana,
Is real Life

To live to serve humanity,
To practise self-restraint,
To control the mind and the senses,
Is real Life

To practise Pranayama,
To do Brahma Vichara,
To stick to resolves.
Is real Life

To live in Om,
To chant Om,
To meditate on Om,
Is real Life

To ignore the names and forms,
To take the essence hidden in them,
To drink the nectar of immortality,
Is real Life

WHAT IS REAL DEATH?

Not to study Gita, Upanishads daily,
Not to remember God at all times,
Not to serve Sadhus and Gurus,
Is real death

Not to have equal vision,
Not to have balanced mind,
Not to have Atma-drishti,
Is real death

Not to have Brahma Jnana.
Not to have a large heart,
Not to do charitable acts,
Is real death

To identify oneself with the body,
To forget one's divine nature,
To live aimlessly,
Is real death

To eat, drink and be merry,
To waste the time uselessly,
To lose one's honour and name,
Is real death

To gamble, and play cards,
To read novels, drink and smoke,
To gossip, cavil and scandalise,
Is real death

To backbite, revile, carry tales
To speak ill of others,
To cheat, falsify and dupe,
Is real death

To earn money unlawfully,
To outrage others' women,
To injure others
Is real death

To lead a sensual life,
To waste vital energy,
To have a lustful look
Is real death

BIRTH AND DEATH

Birth and death are two illusory scenes
In the drama of this world
Really no one is born, no one dies
No one comes, no one goes

It is Maya's jugglery,
It is play of the mind,
Brahman alone exists

There is birth for the body alone,
Five elements combine to form the body,
Atman is birthless and deathless,
Death is casting off the physical sheath

It is like deep sleep
Birth is like waking from sleep,
Be not afraid of death, O Ram!
Life is continuous.

The flower may fade but the fragrance floats,
The body may disintegrate,
But the immortal fragrance of the soul
Always will remain

Learn to discriminate
The Real from the unreal,
Think always of the Infinite
That is birthless and deathless

Transcend Maya and Moha,
Go beyond three Gunas.
Give up attachment for the body
Free yourself from birth and death
And merge in the Immortal Essence

REBIRTH

Rebirth is due to mind
And to the tendencies of the mind
You think and an impression is left in the mind,
This impression is the seed of thought,
The impressions coalesce together
And make tendency or tendencies

As you think
So you become
You take birth
According to your thoughts

Sattva rises upwards,
Rajas is in the middle,
Tamas goes downwards
Enveloped in evil qualities

Mind is the cause
For man's bondage and liberation
An impure mind binds,
A pure mind liberates

When you realise the Truth,
When you know your own Self,
The cause for future births is removed,
The thoughts are killed, the Samskaras are burnt

You are free from rebirth,
You attain Perfection,
You enjoy Supreme Peace,
You become Immortal—This is the Truth

If there is only one birth
If the evil-doer is thrown in eternal fire,
There is no scope for his betterment,
This cannot be accepted.

This is not reasonable too,
Vedanta embraces even the worst sinner,
How sublime is this philosophy !
It proclaims to him

Friends ! Thou art pure Soul,
Sin cannot touch thee,
Regain your lost divinity,
Sin is nothing

Sin is mistake only,
You can destroy sins in the twinkling of an eye,
Be bold, be cheerful,
Stand up, wake up, "Uttishthata, Jagrata"

Gita says "Even the worst sinner
Can become righteous, can cross sins
By the raft of wisdom"
How do you account friend !

For the existence of boy genius,
A child plays on the piano,
A child delivers lectures,
A boy solves great mathematical problems

A child narrates his previous life
One becomes a full-blown Yogi.
This proves that there is rebirth,
Buddha gained experiences in several births

He became Buddha only in his last birth
He who has taste in music,
Gains experiences in several births,
And becomes a master in music in one birth

He cuts grooves for music in each birth,
Slowly develops tendency and aptitude,
And becomes an expert musician in one birth.
So is the case with every Art

The baby sucks, the young duck swims
Who taught this? They are
The Samskaras or the tendencies of previous births
In one birth all virtues cannot be developed.

By gradual evolution only one can cultivate
Saints possess excellence in all virtues,
The existence of saints and adepts
Indicates that there is rebirth

CONTENTS

Chapter Three

RESURRECTION AND JUDGEMENT

Chapter Four

SOUL AFTER DEATH

Chapter Five

DOCTRINE OF REINCARNATION

Chapter Six

LOKAS OR PLANES

Chapter Seven

SPIRITUALISM

Chapter Eight

SHRADDHA AND PRAYER FOR THE DEAD

APPENDIX II

—OM—

What Becomes of The Soul after Death

CHAPTER ONE

WHAT IS DEATH

Death is separation of the Soul from the physical body. Death becomes the starting point of a new and better life Death does not end your personality and self-consciousness It merely opens the door to a higher form of life Death is only the gateway to a fuller life

Birth and death are jugglery of Maya He who is born begins to die He who dies begins to live Life is death and death is life Birth and death are merely doors of entry and exit on the stage of this world In reality no one comes, no one goes Brahman or the Eternal alone exists

Just as you move from one house to another house, the Soul passes from one body to another to gain experience Just as a man casting off worn-out garments, takes new ones, so the dweller in this body, casting off worn-out bodies, enters into others which are new

Death is not the end of life Life is one continuous never-ending process Death is only a passing and a necessary phenomenon, which every Soul has to pass to gain experience for its further evolution.

Dissolution of the body is no more than sleep Just as man sleeps and wakes up, so is death and birth Death is like sleep. Birth is like waking up Death brings promotion to a new and better life A man of discrimination and wisdom is not afraid of death. He knows that death is the gate of life Death to him is no longer a skeleton bearing a sword to cut the thread of life, but rather an angel who has a golden key to unlock for him the door to a wider, fuller and happier existence

Every soul is a circle The circumference of this circle is nowhere but its centre is in the body Death means the change of this centre from body to body Why, then, should you be afraid of death?

The Supreme Soul or Paramatma is deathless, decayless, timeless causeless, spaceless It is the source or substratum for this body, mind and the whole world There is death for the physical body only, which is a compound of five elements How can there be death for the Eternal Soul which is beyond time, space and causation?

If you wish to free yourself from birth and death, you must become bodiless Body is the result of Karmas or actions You must not do any action with expectation of fruits If you free yourself from Raga-dwesha, or likes and dislikes, you will be free from Karma If you kill egoism only, you can free yourself from Raga and Dwesha If you annihilate ignorance through knowledge of the Imperishable, you can annihilate egoism The root-cause for this body is therefore ignorance

He who realises the Eternal Soul, which is beyond all sound, all sight, all taste, all touch, which is formless and attributeless, which is beyond Nature, which is beyond three bodies and five sheaths, which is infinite and unchanging, self-luminous, frees himself from the jaws of death

Death is Not the End of Life

The individual souls or Jivas build various bodies to display their activities and gain experiences from this world They enter the bodies and leave them when they become unfit to live in. They build new bodies again and leave them again in the same manner This is known as transmigration of souls The entrance of a soul into a body is called birth The Soul's departure from the body is called death A body is dead if the Soul is absent.

The conception of a human child in the womb of the mother is the fusion of sperm of man into ovum of woman Spermatozoon and ovum are microscopic living cells They cannot be seen through the naked eye This fusion is generally known as conception and technically as fertilisation of the ovum In the mother's womb sperm (Suklam) and ovum (Sonita) are fused into one single cell This single cell after fertilization develops into an embryo and further in course of ten months into a complete human child

The man has always tried to tear aside the veil and know the course of events subsequent to the death of an individual Various theories have been put forward, but it cannot be said that he has succeeded in tearing aside the veil that covers the life beyond.

Science has been struggling to unravel the mystery, but so far no data has been furnished which can form the basis of a theory But experiments in this direction have yielded many an interesting fact

Natural death, it is said, is unknown to unicellular organisation When life on earth consisted of these creatures, death was unknown The phenomenon appeared only when from unicellular the multicellular evolved

Experiments conducted in laboratories have shown that whole organs such as thyroid glands, the ovary, suprarenal gland, the spleen, the heart and the kidneys isolated from the body of a cat or a fowl, can be kept alive in vitro to show increase in size or weight due to the appearance of new cells or tissues

It is also known that after the cessation of an individuality, parts of the organisation, can continue to function The white blood-corpuscles of the blood, if cared for, can live for months after the body from which they were withdrawn, has been cremated. But the life, it is true, is the life of blood-corpuscles; it is not the life of the individual

Death is not the end of life It is merely the cessation of an important individuality. Life flows on to achieve its conquest of the universal, life flows on till it merges in the Eternal

Process of Death

Vasishtha says in his Yoga Vasishtha

"When on account of the diseases of the body its Nadis lose their vigour and thus become unable to expand and contract in order to exhale or inhale air, the body loses its harmony and becomes restless The inhaled air does not then properly come out, nor does the exhaled air re-enter the body So respiration stops Respiration stopping, the creature becomes senseless and is dead All the desires and ideas of the individual then exist withdrawn within himself The individual with all his Vasanas (desires or previous impressions) within himself is called a Jiva When the body is dead, the Pranas of the individual with the Jiva within, come out of the body and roam in the air The atmospheric air is full of a number of such Pranas which have Jivas within them, these Jivas themselves having their respective world experiences potentially existing within them—I can see them At that time the individual with all his Vasanas within him is called Preta (gone to the other world)

In that very place where one dies, one experiences another world after the insensibility of death is over."

Signs of Death

It is very difficult to find out the real signs of death Stoppage of the heart-beat, stoppage of the pulse or breathing are not the actual signs of death Stoppage of the heart-beat, pulse and respiration, cadaveric rigidity of the limbs, clammy sweat on the body, absence of warmth of the body, are the popular signs of death The doctor tries to find out whether there is corneal reflex in the eye He tries to bend the leg These signs are not the real signs of death, because there have been several cases where there were cessation of breathing and beating of heart and yet they were revived after some time

Hatha Yogis are put in a box and buried underneath the earth for forty days Afterwards they are taken out and they revive Respiration may stop for a long time In cases of suspended animation, respiration stops for two days Many cases have been recorded The heart-beat may stop for many hours, even for days, and then it can be recovered Hence it is extremely difficult to say what would be the actual or the final sign of death The decomposition and putrefaction of the body may be the only final sign of death

No one should be buried immediately after death before decomposition sets in One may think that a man is dead whereas may be in a state of trance, catalepsy or ecstasy or Samadhi Trance, Samadhi, catalepsy and ecstasy are states which resemble death The outward signs are similar

Persons dying of heart-failure should not be buried immediately as breathing would commence once again after a particular time. Burial should take place only after the body begins to putrefy.

A Yogi can stop his heart-beat at his will He can remain in a state of Samadhi, or superconscious state for hours or days There is neither heart-beat nor breathing during the state of Samadhi This is sleepless sleep or perfect awareness When he comes down to physical consciousness, there is revival of heart-beating and respiration Science cannot explain this and doctors are dumb-founded when they witness these phenomena

Dissolution of Elements at Death

This physical body is composed of five great elements or the Mahabhutas, namely, earth water, fire, air and ether The Devas or Gods are endowed with a divine or luminous body The fire Tattwa is predominant in them In man the earth Tattwa is preponderating In the case of aquatic animals the element of water predominates In the case of birds the element of air predominates

Hardness of the body is due to the portion of earth, the fluidity is due to portion of water, the warmth that you feel in the body is due to fire, moving to and fro and such other activities are due to air, space is due to Akasa or ether Jivatma or the individual soul is different from the five elements

After death these elements are dissolved They reach their primordial sources from the inexhaustible storehouse of nature The element of earth goes and joins its storehouse of Prithvi Tattwa The other elements also go back to their sources

The dead body is bathed and newly clothed and is taken to the cremation ground where it is laid on the funeral pyre The Mantras that are now chanted are addressed to the spirit The spirit is invoked to throw out from its body its five Pranas or the vital airs, so that they may mingle with their counterparts in the external air The body is then addressed to dissolve itself with its five material components of earth, water, fire, air and ether from where it originally arose The body is then offered to fire. The spirit which is thus driven out of the body in consequence of the dissolution begins its onward march to the Beyond

The respective functions of the organs are blended with the presiding Gods Sight goes to the Sun from where it had its power of vision, speech goes to the fire, life-breath to the air, the ear into the quarters, the body into the earth, hairs into annual herbs, hairs of the head into trees and blood and semen into waters

Function of Udana Vayu

Vayu is wind or air Vayu is Prana or vital force Prana moves the senses or Indriyas Prana generates thoughts Prana moves the body and causes locomotion Prana digests the food, circulates the blood, excretes urine and motions Prana causes respirations It is through Prana you see, hear, feel, taste and think The sum total of all Pranas is Hiranyagarbha or Lord Brahma Prana is manifestation of Prakritis Gross Prana is breath Subtle Prana is vital force.

Just as there is the subtle bladder within the football, so also there is the subtle body or Sukshma Deha within this gross body Udana Vayu draws out the subtle body from the gross body at the time of death. It is this subtle body that goes to heaven and works in the dreaming state Udana Vayu is the vehicle of transport for all Pranas It helps deglutition or swallowing of food It takes you to Brahman during deep sleep. Its abode is the throat

This immortal Soul or Atman which is the source and support for all the Pranas, mind, intellect, senses and the body abides in the chambers of your heart This Atman is in the heart where there are a hundred and one arteries Every one of these has seventy-two thousand branches Vyana which does the circulation of blood moves in these arteries

Udana which goes up through one of these, leads you to the higher worlds by means of your meritorious actions, to the evil worlds by means of your evil deeds and to the world of men by a mixture of both deeds

In the case of Jivanmuktas or liberated sages who have nothing more by way of births nor worlds to live in, their minds and Pranas get absorbed in Brahman The individual soul merges itself in the supreme soul or Para Brahman

In the Jivanmuktas there is no question of any forerunner like the Udana Vayu The liberated sages with their minds purified by renunciation and with knowledge of the imperishable Atman are completely absorbed at the time of death There is no return to this world for them

What is Soul?

There are two kinds of Soul viz, the individual Soul or Jivatma or the human Soul, and the Supreme Soul or Paramatma The individual Soul is an image or reflection of the Supreme Soul Just as the Sun is reflected in different parts of water, so also the Supreme Soul is reflected in different minds of different persons

Soul is spirit It is immaterial. It is intelligence or consciousness It is Chaitanya Individual soul is reflected Chaitanya It is this individual soul that departs from the body after its death and goes to heaven with the senses, mind Prana, impressions desires and tendencies It is endowed with a subtle astral body when it proceeds to heaven

When the water in the lake is absorbed the reflection of the Sun in the water merges in the Sun itself Even so when the mind is annihilated through meditation, the individual soul merges itself in the Supreme Soul or Paramatma. This is the goal of life

The individual soul has become impure through cravings, desires, egoism, pride, greed, lust and likes and dislikes Hence it is finite (Paricchinna), it is endowed with limited knowledge (Alpajna) and limited power (Alpa Saktiman) The Supreme Soul is Infinite Omniscient and Omnipotent It is an embodiment of knowledge and bliss

The individual soul is under bondage through ignorance and limiting adjuncts such as mind, body and senses It is mere appearance It is illusory When it attains knowledge of the Imperishable it is freed from limiting adjuncts and bondage Just as the bubble becomes one with the ocean, so also the Jiva becomes one with the Supreme Soul when ignorance is destroyed

A dead body cannot speak, cannot walk, cannot see It remains like a log of wood after the soul has departed from the body It is the soul that enlivens, galvanises moves and directs the body, mind and the senses

The Supreme Soul is self-consciousness, self awareness, self-delight, self-knowledge, self-existence It knows itself and knows others It is self-luminous and illumines everything Hence it is Chaitanya Matter does not know itself It does not know others Hence it is Jada or insentient

The Supreme Soul is formless, attributeless, all-pervading, indivisible, decayless, timeless, spaceless. There is neither time nor day nor night in the Sun itself, although it creates day and night So is the Supreme Soul Soul is Infinite, Eternal, Immortal

The Supreme alone exists This world of names and forms is illusory. It is superimposed upon the Supreme Soul, just as snake is superimposed on the rope Bring a light, the snake in the rope vanishes at once Attain illumination or knowledge of the Supreme Soul This world will vanish in toto

Everybody feels 'I exist'. 'I am, Aham Asmi' No one can say 'I do not exist' This itself proves the existence of an Immortal Soul or the Supreme Self In deep sleep you rest in the Supreme Soul There is no world for you You enjoy unalloyed bliss This proves that the Supreme Soul exists and its essential nature is pure bliss

Purify your mind Steady it Fix the mind on the Supreme Soul Meditate and realise your essential divine nature You will be freed from the wheel of births and deaths You will attain eternal bliss and immortality

Philosophy of Flesh

Charvakas are atheists who deny the existence of the Soul after the death of the body The materialists who worship the body as the soul and who deny the existence of a soul independent of the body, which is separate from the body, are also atheists. The Charvakas, the Lokayatikas and the materialists believe that the body only is the soul and that the soul does not exist outside the body. They also believe that the soul dies when the body dies

They say that the soul is formed by the combination of the five elements just as the red colour is formed by the combination of betel leaves, nuts and lime, or just as an intoxicating liquor is formed by the combination of some ingredients Is this not a beautiful philosophy? It is the philosophy of the flesh It is the philosophy of Virochana and his followers

They believe in nothing which cannot be cognised by the senses They will not admit the existence of anything which lies beyond the reach of their senses They want occular proof for everything They must see the soul with the naked eyes Then only they will believe in the existence of a soul They do not know that the soul can be intuitively realised and that it is not an object of perception Their philosophy is "Eat, drink and be merry Have sensual enjoyment to maximum degree Do not think of the future If you have no money, beg or borrow it and then eat and drink Then again drink, because when the body is burnt to ashes, no one will have to be accountable for your actions" Such philosophers are abundant in every country Their number is increasing daily There are many who do not believe at all in the existence of a soul.

The Charvakas and the materialists do not bother about reincarnation or transmigration of souls, about philosophical questions like "Who am I? Whence and where? Whither? What remains after death? What is life? What is death? What is then on the other side of death? When the body dies what conditions shall man pass into, in which world shall he find himself?" They think that those who make such enquiries are ignorant persons and that they are the only clever and wise persons No argument can convince them or change their views They have written volumes after volumes against the existence of the soul Wonderful people indeed with perverted intellects!

Most of the modern college-students of India, the children of the ancient Rishis and Seers of India have become followers of the above philosophy on account of wrong education and wrong association They are in the grip of the devil They are in the clutches of fashion and passion They have left off prayer, Sandhya, Gayatri Japa, Satsanga, study of Gita and Upanishads, Ramayana and Bhagavatam They are worshippers of the body They practise vile imitation in dress etc They visit hotels, restaurants, clubs and cinemas regularly, play cards and study novels enthusiastically They have no idea of the financial difficulties of their parents and spend hundreds monthly After graduation they cannot earn even fifty Ignorant parents foolishly imagine that their sons will become big judges, big engineers, barristers and civilians and educate them even by borrowing money and selling their lands They eventually find them in the role of unemployment Nature surely punishes wicked students.

The Charvakas and materialists hold that the

combination of matter or body produces thought, intelligence, consciousness, mind and soul, and that consciousness etc , lasts so long as the body lasts They believe that thought or intelligence or consciousness is a function or secretion of the brain, just as bile is a secretion of the liver Very strange indeed! Combination of atoms and molecules can never generate thought, intelligence or consciousness Motion cannot produce sensation, ideas and thoughts Consciousness or intelligence is verily not an act of motion No scientist can prove that matter or force has ever produced consciousness or intelligence The Charvakas and the materialists are deluding themselves by various false arguments They have lost their power of discrimination on account of sensual indulgence They have not got the subtle pure intellect to discern things in their proper light Consciousness, intelligence and bliss are the attributes of the Universal Soul This body is constantly changing This physical body, which is a combination of the five elements, will be destroyed But the eternal Soul which is the basis, substratum and source for matter, energy, mind, will ever remain The sense of 'I' will continue to exist even after this body perishes You can never think or imagine that you do not exist after the body is destroyed There is an innate feeling in you that you do exist after the body is gone. This proves that there is an immortal soul independent of the body The soul can never be demonstrated, but its existence can be inferred by certain empirical facts

The innate question "What remains after death? What becomes of the soul after the death of the body?

Where is he gone? Does he still exist?" spontaneously arises in all minds This is a momentous question which touches the hearts of all deeply The same question arises today in all people of all countries, as it arose thousands of years ago No one can stop this The same question is discussed today and it will be discussed in the future also From ancient times, philosophers, sages, saints, Yogins, thinkers, Swamis, metaphysicians and prophets have tried their best to solve this great problem

When you lead a life of luxury, when you are rolling in wealth, you forget it But the moment you see that one of your dearest relations is snatched away by the cruel hand of death you are struck with awe and wonder and begin to reflect within yourself. "Where is he gone? Does he still exist? Is there a soul independent of body? He cannot be totally annihilated His impressions of thoughts and actions cannot die".

The seers of the Upanishads boldly declare with emphasis on account of their intuitive realisation, that there is One All-pervading Immortal Soul, Self-luminous All-Blissful, Birthless, Decayless, Deathless, Timeless, Spaceless, Thoughtless, and that the Individual Soul is identical with this Supreme Soul when his limiting adjuncts such as body and mind are dissolved, when he is freed from ignorance through knowledge of the Imperishable Soul. Soul is the Inner Ruler and Director of the mind, Prana and the senses Mind borrows its light from the Soul

Soul is beyond the realm of physical science. Soul is beyond the reach of material science. Man is a soul wearing a physical body Soul is extremely subtle It is subtler than ether, mind and energy Consciousness, intelligence are of the soul and not of the body Consciousness is evidence of the existence of the Soul Personality of man is a brief, partial manifestation of the Immortal, All-pervading, Indivisible Soul or Atman or Brahman Soul is the immortal part in man O ignorant man, who has been led astray by the study of those books which deny the existence of an immortal Soul, wake up now from the slumber of ignorance Open your eyes You have already reserved a seat for you in hell and obtained a direct passport to this dark region by study of heaven-closing, worthless books Burn these books at once and study Gita and Upanishads Do Japa, Kirtan and meditation regularly and thoroughly overhaul your wrong Samskaras Then only you are saved from destruction

Do not identify with this body. You are not this perishable body You are the immortal Soul Identify yourself with the Soul "Tat Twam Asi" 'Thou art That' Feel this Realise this and be free

Swoon, Sleep, Death

A man lying in a swoon cannot be said to be awake because he does not perceive external objects by means of his senses. The man who returns to consciousness from a swoon says "I was shut up in blind darkness, I was conscious of nothing" A wakeful man keeps his body upright but the body of a swooning person falls down

He is not dreaming, because he is altogether unconscious Nor is he dead as he has life and warmth He continues to breathe

When a man has become senseless and people are in doubt whether he is alive or dead, they touch the region of the heart in order to find out whether there is warmth in his body or not and put their hands to his nostrils to find out whether there is breathing or not If they find out there is neither warmth nor breath they come to the conclusion that he is dead If they perceive warmth and breath they decide that he is not dead and begin to sprinkle cold water on his face so that he may recover consciousness

He who has swooned is not dead, because he rises again to conscious life

A man who has swooned may sometimes not breathe for a long time His body trembles, his face is dreadful His eyes are staring wide open But a sleeping man looks calm and happy He draws his breath at regular intervals His eyes are closed His body does not tremble A sleeping man may be aroused by a gentle stroking with the hand but a person lying in a swoon cannot be aroused even by a blow with a stick Swoon is due to external causes It is caused by a blow on the head with a stick or the like; while sleep is due to fatigue Swoon is half sleep It does not mean by this that he half enjoys Brahman. It means that it partly resembles sleep The man who lies in a swoon belongs with one half to the side of deep sleep, while the other half to the side of death. In fact swoon is the door to death If there is a remnant of Karma he returns to consciousness. Else, he dies.

The state of swoon is recognised by the Ayurveda and Allopathic doctors. It is known from ordinary experience.

The silent witness of waking state, dreaming state, deep sleep state and swoon is Brahman, thy innermost Self, Immortal Atman or the Inner Ruler. Identify yourself with Brahman, transcend all the states and be ever happy and blissful.

CHAPTER TWO

SOUL'S JOURNEY AFTER DEATH

The Jiva or the individual Soul along with the Pranas, the mind and the senses leaves his former body and obtains a new body. He takes with himself Avidya, virtues and vicious actions and the impressions left by his previous births

Just as a caterpillar takes hold of another object before it leaves its hold of an object, so also, the Soul has the vision of the body to come, before it leaves the present body Hence the view of the Sankhyas, that the Self and the organs are both all-pervading and when obtaining a new body only begin to function in it on account of Karma, the view of the Bauddhas, that the Soul alone without the organs begins to function in a new body, new senses being formed like the new body, the view of the Vaiseshikas that the mind alone goes to the new body and the view of the Digambara Jains that the Soul only flies away from the old body and alights in the new one just as a parrot flies from one tree to another, are not correct and are opposed to the Vedas The Soul goes from the body accompanied by the mind, Prana, the senses and the Sukshmabhutas or elements

The Soul takes with it the subtle parts of the elements which are the seeds of the new body All the elements accompany the Soul

When he departs, the chief Prana departs after him and when the Prana thus departs, all the other Pranas depart after it They cannot stay without the basis or substratum or support of the elements The subtle elements or Tanmatras form the base for the moving of Pranas

There can be enjoyment only when the Prana goes to another body The essence of the elements is the vehicle of the Pranas Where the elements are, there the organs and Pranas are They are never separated The Soul could not enter into the new body without Prana

The Pranas and the senses remain at the time of death quite inoperative for accompanying the departing Soul

The materials like milk, curd, etc, that are offered as oblations in sacrifices assume a subtle form called Apurva and attach themselves to the sacrificer The Jivas then go enveloped by water which is supplied by the materials that are offered as oblations in sacrifices

The water forming the oblation assumes the subtle form of Apurva, envelopes the Souls and leads them to Heaven to receive their rewards

Those who perform sacrifices give enjoyment to the gods in Heaven and rejoice with them They become serviceable companions to the gods They contribute to the enjoyment of the gods by their presence and service in that world They enjoy in the Chandraloka and return to the earth at the end of their store of merit

The Souls that descend from heaven have a remnant of Karma which determines their birth The Souls return to the earth by the force of some unenjoyed remnants of Karma When the totality of works which helped the Souls to go to the Chandraloka for enjoyment of the fruits of good deeds is exhausted, then the body made up of water which had originated there for the sake of enjoyment is dissolved by the fire of sorrow springing from the thought that the enjoyment comes to an end, just as hailstones melt by contact with the rays of the sun, just as ghee melts by contact with fire Then the Souls come down with a remainder yet left

We read in Chandogya Upanishad V 107 "Those whose conduct during the previous life has been good presently obtain good birth, such as the birth of a Brahmin, a Kshatriya, or a Vaisya, those whose conduct has been bad presently obtain some evil birth such as that of a dog or a pig"

The Smriti says "The members of the different castes and of the different orders of life who are engaged in the works prescribed for them, after leaving this world and enjoying the fruits of their works in other world, are born again owing to the unenjoyed portion of their rewards, in distinguished castes and families, with special beauty, longevity, knowledge, conduct, property, comfort and intelligence" Hence the Soul is born with residual Karma.

Some capital sins like the killing of a Brahmin involve many births The Soul descends by the route by which he went to a certain stage and then by a different route

The sinners do not go to Chandraloka They go to Yama Loka or the world of punishment and after having experienced the results of their evil deeds come down to the earth

Hells are places of torture for the evil doers The temporary abodes are Raurava, Maharaurava, Vahni, Vaitarani and Kumbhika The two eternal hells are Tamisra (darkness) and Andhatamisra (blinding darkness) The seven hells are superintended by Chitragupta and others Yama is the chief ruler in those seven hells also Chitragupta and others are only Superintendents and Lieutenants empolyed by Yama They are all under Yama's government and suzerainty Chitragupta and others are directed by Yama

The Third Place

The Sruti says that those who do not go by means of Vidya along the path of Devayana to Brahmaloka or by means of Karma along the path of Pitriyana tò Chandraloka are born often in low bodies and die often The evil-doers go to the third place (Tritiyam sthanam) The Sruti passage says "Now those who go along neither of these ways become those small creatures, flies, worms, etc, continually returning, of whom it may be said "Live and Die" Theirs is the third place. The sinners are called small creatures because they assume the bodies of insects, gnats, etc Their place is called the third place because it is neither Brahmaloka, nor the Chandraloka

The souls return the way they went, to the ether, from ether to air Then the sacrificer having become air becomes smoke, having become smoke he becomes mist, having become mist, he becomes cloud, having become cloud he rains down The Souls do not attain identity with ether, air, etc They become only like ether, air, etc They assume a subtle form like ether, come under the influence or power of air and get mixed or connected with smoke etc The Soul passes through them quickly

"Having become cloud he rains down Then he is born as rice, corn, herbs, tree, sesamum and beans. From them the escape is beset with most difficulties For, whoever the person may be who eats the food and begets offspring he henceforth becomes like unto them" Ch Up 10 5

The soul's journey through the stages of the ether, air, vapour or smoke, mist, cloud and rain takes shorter time than his passing through the stages of corn semen, foetus, which takes a much longer time of hard suffering

Naradeeya Purana says "He who has begun to descend will enter the mother's womb before a year passes since starting, though wandering through different places"

The Souls are merely connected with rice and plants which are already animated by other Souls and do not enjoy their pleasures and pains They become connected with those plants

The Souls use the rice and plants as their halting station without being identified with them They do not lose their identity

Chandogya Upanishad declares "Whoever eats the food and performs the act of generation, that again the Soul becomes" (V 10 6) The Soul gets connected with one who performs the act of generation The descending Soul becomes again that food and that semen The Soul remains in him, in copulation only till he enters into the mother's womb with the semen injected He has a touch with the seminal fluid created by eating such grain and ultimately attains a body in the womb

He attains a fully developed human body in the womb of the mother which is fit for experiencing the fruits of the remainder of works The family on which he is to be born is regulated by the nature of the remainder as mentioned in Ch Up V 10-7 "Of these, those whose conduct here has been good will quickly attain good birth, the birth of a Brahmana, or a Kshatriya or a Vaisya But those, whose, conduct here has been bad will quickly attain an evil birth, of a dog, or a hog, or Chandala"

The whole object of teaching this law of incarnation is that you should realise that the Atman or the Absolute alone is the highest bliss The Atman alone must be your sole object of quest You should get disgusted with this world of pain and sorrow and develop dispassion, discrimination and try earnestly to attain the eternal bliss of the Absolute

O ignorant man! O foolish man! O miserable man! O deluded Soul! Wake up from your long slumber of ignorance Open your eyes Develop the four means of salvation and attain the goal of life, the *summum bonum*, right now, in this very birth. Come out of this cage of flesh You have been long imprisoned in this prison-house of body from time immemorial You have been dwelling in the womb again and again Cut the knot of Avidya and soar high in the realms of eternal Bliss

Karma and Reincarnation (i)

Death is the separation of the Soul from the body All the sorrow of man comes from the body. The sage has no fear of death, because he identifies himself with the All-pervading, Immortal Soul

Karma and rebirth are the two great pillars of Hinduism and Buddhism too He who does not believe in these two great truths cannot grasp the essence of these two religions

You can overcome pain and sorrow, if you know the meaning of sorrow, pain, suffering and death The phenomenon of death sets the human mind to think deeply All philosophy springs from the phenomenon of death Philosophy is really study of death The highest philosophy in India starts with the subject of death Study Bhagavad Gita, Kathopanishad and the Chandogya Upanishad, which treat of this Death is a call to reflect and to seek the goal of Truth, the Eternal Brahman

Death is nothing but the change of body The Soul throws it off like a used garment. Human life is getting purged and perfected in order to attain the final bliss This takes place through myriads of births

According to Hinduism, life is one continuous never-ending process All change is only change of environment and embodiment The Soul is Immortal It takes one form after another on account of its own actions Hinduism is based on two fundamental doctrines, viz the Law of Karma and the law of transmigration Death is only a necessary and passing phenomenon Just as you move from one house to another, the Soul passes from one body to another to gain experiences

The Soul which passes out of the body after death is termed "Preta", one that is bound on its onward march to the Beyond The Soul in its disembodied form hovers about its original and familiar places for ten days It is in the form of a ghost during these ten days The astral body takes shape from day to day with the formation of the head, eyes and other limbs of the Linga Sarira, fed and nourished by the sesamum and water poured out in libation over the stones which represent the ancestors

Soul is fully embodied on the eleventh day It starts on its journey to the judgment seat of Lord Yama, the God of death. It takes one full year from the time of death to reach Lord Yama's place The path is beset with obstacles, distress and difficulties The man who has done most wicked deeds suffers more But the difficulties can be removed and the journey be rendered easy and comfortable by the oblations and offerings given by the son of the deceased during the first year of the Soul's journey and by feeding pure and learned Brahmins The son should offer rice balls to the father, without weeping Death is certain for those who are born, and birth is certain for the dead This is inevitable Therefore, you should not grieve over it The ten days' rites should not be neglected The son should perform the Sapinda ceremony on the twelfth day and the sixteen monthly offerings The Soul is sustained on its onward march to the judgment seat by the libations offered to it by the son

The Soul is scorched on the way by intense heat, but the gift of an unbrella by his son on the eleventh day gives pleasant shade above his head The path is full of great thorns, but the gift of shoes helps him to go riding on horses The miseries of cold, heat and wind are dreadful there, but he goes happily along the way by the power of gift of clothes There is great heat and there is no water, but drinks water when thirsty, through the gift of a water-pot by his son The son should make a gift of a cow

Chitragupta, the recorder of fate, the Accountant General in the Kingdom of Lord Yama, informs the Soul of his good and bad actions in his earthly life after the end of one full year The Soul leaves off its Pretatwa or the garb of a traveller on this day He is raised to the status of a Pitri or Ancestor

Ancestor worship is one of the fundamental doctrines of Hinduism There are three stages in the ancestral life viz, father, grandfather and great-grandfather and mother, grandmother and great-grandmother These are the ancestors to any one living here He who has done meritorious actions on this earth-life becomes united with his ancestors in the Pitri-loka and lives with them.

Those who have given up the performance of Sraaddha, Tarpan and other religious rites on account of wrong influence ignorance and egoism have done great harm to their ancestors and themselves They should wake up now They should start doing these ceremonies from now It is not too late now

May you all obtain the blessings of your ancestors through performance of anniversaries and other rites, and regular ancestor-worship

How Soul Departs After Death

At the time of death when the breathing becomes difficult the Jiva or the Self that is in the body goes out making noises Just as a cart heavily loaded goes on creaking, so does the Jiva creak while the Prana departs

The Jiva or the individual self has the subtle body as its limiting adjunct It moves between this and the next world as between the waking and the dream states It moves from birth to death While in birth it associates itself with the physical body and the organs, in death it disassociates with them The departure of the Soul is immediately followed by the departure of the vital force It is presided over by the supreme self-luminous Atman. It is through the light of the Self that the man sits, moves and does his daily duties

The subtle body has the vital force or Prana as its chief constituent It is revealed by the self-luminous Atman When the subtle body rises up, the Atman also seems to go with it Otherwise how can the Self being unified with the Supreme Self, go making noises like a cart? It goes making noises because it is afflicted by the pain as the vital parts are being slashed Loss of memory is caused as a result of this vital and excruciating pain He is then put in a helpless state of mind on account of the pangs felt Therefore, he is unable to adopt the requisite means for his well-being, before that crisis comes He must be alert in practising the means conducive to that end He is not able to think of God

In old age, the body becomes thin and emaciated on account of fever and other diseases When the body is extremely emaciated by fever and other causes, dyspnoea sets in and at this stage the man goes making noises like the overloaded cart

The causes of death are many and indefinite Man is ever in the jaws of death Death overtakes him suddenly when he is the least prepared for it. He ever thinks that he will escape death or even if he believes in death to be certain he expects it only at a very distant date Just as the mango, fig or the fruit of the Pepul tree is detached from its stalk, so does this infinite being completely detaching himself from the parts of the body, again go in the same way that he came to particular bodies, for the unfoldment of his vital force The self that is identified with the subtle body completely detaches itself from the parts of the body such as the eye, etc He is not able to preserve the body through the vital force at the time of his departure Just as he detaches himself from the body and the organs, and enters deep sleep, even so, he detaches himself from this body during death and attaches himself to another. As frequently as man moves from the dreaming to the waking, from the waking to the dream and thence to deep sleep, so frequently does he transmigrate from one body to another. He has transmigrated from many such bodies in the past and will continue to do so in future as well He gets his future birth according to his past work, knowledge and so forth He goes from one body to another, only for the unfoldment of the vital force It is by this vital force, that he fulfils his object viz, the enjoyment of the fruits of his work The vital force is only auxiliary to the enjoyment of the fruits of his work and hence the specification "For the unfoldment of his vital force"

The Jiva has adopted the whole universe as his means to the realisation of the fruits of his work and he is going from one body to another to fulfil this object Therefore the whole universe implied by his work waits for him with the requisite means for the realisation of the fruits of his work made ready The Satapatha Brahmana says, "A man is born into the body that has been made for him" (VI-ii 2 27) It is analogous to the case of a man about to return from the dream to the waking state

The Departing Soul Compared to a King

When the king of a country pays a visit to some place within his kingdom, the leaders of the particular village anticipating the king's arrival wait on him with varieties of food, drink, beautiful mansions for his stay etc. They say, "Here he comes, here he comes" So also the elements and the presiding deities, Indra and the rest who help the organs to function, wait upon the departing Self with the means of enjoying the fruits of his work. They secure for him a suitable body to enjoy the fruits of his action

When the king wishes to depart, the particular leaders of the village approach him unbidden simply by knowing that he wishes to go, so do all the organs approach the departing man, the experiencer of the fruits of his work, at the time of death. The organs approach him when the breathing becomes difficult knowing that he wishes to depart. They do not go at the command of the departing Self They go of their own accord knowing the wish of their commander

Process of Detachment

It has already been stated that the self completely detaches itself from the body and the organs at the time of death When the self becomes weak and senseless the organs come to it It is not the Self that becomes weak, it is the body But the weakness of the self is figuratively spoken of. The Self being formless can never by itself become weak So is the case with senselessness The state of helplessness noticeable at the time of death, which is caused by the withdrawal of the organs, is attributed by people to the Self So they say, "Oh, he has become senseless!"

When the man is about to die, the various organs withdraw themselves into their original source and help no more the function of the organs. In death there is a complete withdrawal of the organs into the heart or the heart lotus or Akasa of the heart. But in the state of dream the organs are not absolutely withdrawn Here lies the difference between sleep and death

In the case of the organ eye, the being associated with the eye who is a part of the Sun, goes on helping the functions of the eye, as he lives When he dies he ceases to help the eye and is merged in his own Self the sun In like manner, all the organs merge themselves in their respective presiding deities e g , speech in Fire, the vital force in Vayu etc The respective organs together with their presiding deities occupy their respective places when the man takes another body This merging and reappearing takes place every day during sleep When the presiding deity of the eye turns back from all sides, the dying man fails to notice colour At this time the self completely withdraws the particles of light, as in the dream state

Every organ becomes united with the subtle body of the dying man It is then, people at his side say of him, "He does not see now" Thus when one by one all the presiding deities or organs withdraw and merge into the cause, the respective organ stops functioning Then the dying man hears not, sees not, smells not, speaks not and becomes senseless He loses his consciousness for ever. He never remembers he is Mr So-and-so and that he belongs to such-and-such a caste, etc He loses his understanding, memory and waking consciousness The external world becomes void for him The organs are then united in the heart

In the subtle body the self-effulgent intelligence of the Atman is always particularly manifest It is because of this limiting adjunct that the Self comes under relative existence involving all such changes as birth and death and going and coming

How the Self Departs

The passage of the self from the body varies according to the number of good actions done by the Jiva and the knowledge gained by him If he has a good store of virtuous deeds and relative knowledge that would take him to the Sun, the self leaves the body through the eye It leaves through the head if he is entitled to the world of Hiranyagarbha It leaves through other passages according to its past work and knowledge

When the individual self departs for the next world the vital force or Prana also departs When Prana departs all the other organs too depart The self has particular consciousness as in dreams in consequence of its past work It does not have independent consciousness. If it had independent consciousness everybody would achieve the end of his life A man attains whatever he thinks of at the moment of death if he has always been imbued with that idea Everybody has at the moment a consciousness which consists of impressions in the form of particular modifications of the mind He goes to the body which is related to that consciousness. Therefore, in order to have freedom of action at the time of death, those aspirants who desire emancipation should be very alert in the practice of Yoga and right knowledge and the acquisition of merits during their lifetime

The self journeying to the next world is followed by knowledge of all sorts It has the full knowledge of both the works enjoined and prohibited It carries the impressions of experiences regarding every action that it performed in the past incarnations These impressions play an active part in moulding the character of the Jiva in the next birth His fresh actions in the next birth are motivated by the impressions of actions of past life The senses attain skill in performing certain works even without much practice in this life It is observed generally that some are very skilful in painting They can excel the best painter even without any practice There are others who cannot do the same work even after much practice All this is due to the revival or non-revival of the past impressions

Knowledge, work and past experience are the three factors in deciding the future of an individual One should, therefore, cultivate virtues, perform good actions so that he may attain a desirable and agreeable body with desirable enjoyments

The organs are all-pervading and all-comprising Their limitation in the sphere of the body and the elements is due to the work, knowledge and past experiences of men Therefore, although the organs are naturally all-pervading and infinite, since the new body is made in accordance with the person's work, knowledge and past impressions, the functions of the organs also contract or expand accordingly.

Just as a leech supported on a straw goes to the end of it, takes hold of another support and contracts itself, so does the self throw his body aside, make it senseless, take hold of another support and contract itself

Just as a goldsmith takes apart a little quantity of gold and fashions another, a newer and better form, so does the self throw this body away, or make it senseless and make another, a newer and better form, suited for the enjoyments in the world of the Manes, Celestials, Gods or Hiranyagarbha

Desire is the root-cause of transmigration Being attached to the desires the individual soul attains that result to which his subtle body or mind is attached Exhausting the results of whatever work he did in this life, he returns from that world to this for fresh work Thus, does the man who desires to transmigrate But the man who does not desire never transmigrates He who is free from desires, the objects of whose desires have been attained and to whom all objects of desire are but the Self—the organs do not depart, being but Brahman, he is merged in Brahman To a knower of Brahman who has routed out his desires, work will produce no baneful result, for the Sruti says 'For one who has completely attained the objects of his desire and realised the self, all desires dissolve in this very life'—Mundaka Upanishad

Soul's Journey After Death

The soul accompanied by the chief vital air (Mukhya-Prana), the sense-organs and the mind and taking with itself Avidya, good and evil actions and the impressions left by his previous existences, leaves its former body and obtains a new body

When the soul passes from one body to another he is enveloped by the subtle parts of the elements which are the seeds of the new body.

He rises on the road leading through the smoke and so on, to the sphere of the moon After enjoying the fruits of his good actions he again descends to the earth with a remainder of the works, by the way he went and differently too

When the Karma, which gave the soul a birth as a god in heaven, is exhausted the remaining Karma, good or bad brings him back to the earth Otherwise it is difficult to explain the happiness or misery of a new-born child

It is not possible that in one life the entire Karma of the previous life is worked out Because a man might have done both good and bad deeds, as a result of which he is born as a god, or an animal The working out of both kinds of Karmas simultaneously in one birth is not possible Hence although the result of virtuous actions is exhausted by the enjoyment of heaven, there are other Karmas in store according to which a man is born again in good or bad environments

The soul has a vision of the body to come Just as a leech or caterpillar takes hold of another object before it leaves its hold of an object, the Soul visualises the body to come, before he leaves the present body.

The view that after death the entire store of Karmas about to bear fruit fructifies and that hence, those who return from Chandraloka do so without any remainder of work, is wrong Supposing that some of those Karmas can be enjoyed only in one kind of birth and some in another, how could they combine in one birth? We cannot say that one portion ceases to bear fruit. There is no such cessation except by Prayaschitta or expiation If the entire Karmas bear fruit, there will be no cause for rebirth after life in heaven or hell or in animal bodies because in these there is no means of Dharma or Adharma Moreover, some sins like the killing of a Brahmin involve many births Sri Madhvacharya writes in his Bhashya of Brahma Sutras that from the fourteenth year of age the jiva does of necessity works, each of which would be the cause of at least ten births How then can the entirety of Karmas lead to one birth alone?

The Two Paths—Devayana and Pitriyana

The Path of Light (Devayana)

The Uttara Marga or Devayana path or northern path or the path of light is the path by which the Yogins go to Brahman This path leads to salvation This path takes the devotee to Brahmaloka Having reached the path of the gods he comes to the world of Agni, to the world of Vayu, to the world of Varuna to the world of Indra, to the world of Prajapati, to the world of Brahman

They go to light, from light to day, from day to the waxing half of the moon, from the waxing half of the moon to the six months when the Sun goes to the north, from those six months to the year, from the year to the Aditya

When the person goes away from this world he comes to Vayu Then Vayu makes room for him like the hole of a wheel and through it he mounts higher till he comes to Aditya.

From the moon to the lightning there is a person, not a man (Amanava Purusha), who leads him to Brahman

The bright path is the path,to the Devas, Devayana, of the devotees; the bright path is open to the devotees

The Path of Darkness (Pitriyana)

The Pitriyana path or the path of darkness or the path of ancestors leads to rebirth Those who do sacrifices to gods, and other charitable works with expectation of fruits go to the Chandraloka through this path and come back to this world when their fruits of Karmas are exhausted.

There are smoke and dark-coloured objects throughout the course There is no illumination when one passes along this path It is reached by Avidya or ignorance Hence it is called the path of darkness or smoke The dark path is to the Pitris or forefathers—Pitriyana of the Karmins who do sacrifices or charitable acts with expectation of fruits

These two paths are not open to the whole world. The bright path is open to the devotees and the dark path to the Karmins. Samsara is eternal and so the paths also are eternal

The Pranas of Jivanmuktas who have attained knowledge of the self do not depart. They are absorbed in Brahman. The Jivanmuktas who attain Kaivalya-Moksha or immediate salvation have no place to go to or to return from. They become one with the All-pervading Brahman.

Knowing the nature of the two paths and the consequence they lead to, the Yogi never loses his discrimination. The Yogi who knows that the path of Devayana or the path of lights leads to Moksha (Karma Mukti) and the path of darkness to Samsara or the world of births and deaths, is no longer deluded. Knowledge of these two paths serves as a compass or a beacon-light to guide the Yogi's steps at every moment.

CHAPTER THREE

RESURRECTION AND JUDGMENT

Resurrection

Resurrection is rising again from the dead Resurrection judgment by God reward or punishment are the three important tenets of Mohammedanism, Christianity and Zoroastrianism

The Jews who lent this doctrine to the Christians and Mohammedans, themselves borrowed it from the Parsis

According to some writers the resurrection will be merely spiritual The general opinion, however, is that both body and the soul will be raised from the grave It may be asked how will the body which has been decomposed rise again? But Mohammed has taken care to preserve one part of the body to serve as a basis for future edifice, or rather a leaven for the mass which is to be joined to it He taught that a man's body was entirely consumed by the earth, except only the bone called Al Ajib or the coccygis or rump bone It was the first-formed in the human body It will also remain uncorrupted till the last day as a seed from which the whole is to be renewed.

Mohammed said that this would be ~~been taken~~ a forty day's rain which God would send, and ~~men-~~ would cover the earth to the height of twelve cubits ~~ay,~~ and cause the bodies to sprout forth like plants

The Jews also say the same thing of the bone Luz, but they say that tne body would sprout by a dew impregnating the dust of the earth

In 31st chapter of the Bundehesh,the question is asked "How will the body which the wind has carried away and the waves have swallowed be re-created, how will the resurrection of the dead take place?" To this replied Ormuzd "When through me the corn which is laid in the earth grows again and comes once more to life, when I have given to the trees veins according to their kinds, when I have placed the child in the mother, when I have created the clouds which take up the water of the earth and send it down again in rain where I will, when I have created each and all of these things, would it be harder for me to bring about the resurrection? Remember, all this has been once and I have created it and can I not re-create what has already been lost?"

The simile of the seed of corn which is laid in the lap of the mother earth and afterwards shoots out into countless blades is often instanced as a proof of the Resurrection "When the seed of the wheat was buried naked in the earth springs up in the manifold clothings of the blades, how much more will the virtuous rise again, who have been interred in their vestments?" Three keys lie in the hands of God and are entrusted to no delegate These are (1) the

.ain, (2) that of birth, and (3) that .esurrection. Signs of Resurrection The .ach of the day of resurrection will be known om certain signs which are to precede it They are (1) The rising of the Sun in the west, (2) The appearance of Dajal, a monster of most curious appearance who will preach the truth of Islam in Arabic language, (3) The blast of the trumpet called Sur, which will be sounded three times

All these are more or less Jewish ideas After the resurrection, and before the Judgment, the resuscitated souls will have to wait for a long time under the burning heat of the Sun, which will descend to within a few yards of their heads

The Day of Judgment

The departed soul will wait for some time Then God will appear to judge them. Mohammed will take the office of intercessor Then everyone will be examined regarding all his actions in his life All the limbs and parts of the body will be made to confess the sins committed by each Each person will be given a book in which all his actions are recorded. This corresponds to the book of the Hindus in which Chitragupta, the Superintendent of Lord Yama, records all the actions of human beings

Gabriel will hold a balance and the books will be weighed in the balance Those, whose virtuous deeds are heavier than the evil ones, will be sent to heaven Those, whose wicked deeds are heavier than their good actions, will be sent to hell

This belief of the Mohammedans has been taken from the Jews The old Jewish writers have mentioned of the books to be produced at the last day, which contain a record of men's deeds and the balance wherein they shall be weighed

The Jews borrowed this idea from the Zoroastrians The Zoroastrians hold that two angels named Mehr and Sarush will stand on the bridge on the day of Judgment to examine every person as he passes Mehr represents divine mercy. He will hold a balance in his hand to weigh the actions of men. God will pronounce the sentence in accordance with the report of Mehr. If the good actions preponderate, if they turn the scale even by the weight of a hair, they will be sent to heaven But those whose good deeds will be found light, will be thrown from the bridge into hell by the other angel, Sarush, who represents Justice of God

There is a bridge called Al Sirat by Mohammed, which is on the road to heaven. This bridge is thrown over the abyss of hell This bridge is finer than hair and sharper than the edge of a sword Those Mohammedans, who have done good deeds, will easily cross this bridge Mohammed will lead them The evildoers will miss their footing and fall down headlong into the hell, which is gaping beneath them

The Jews speak of the bridge of hell which is not broader than a thread. The Hindus speak of Vaitarani The Zoroastrians teach that all men will have to pass over the bridge called Pul Chinavat on the last day

CHAPTER FOUR

SOUL AFTER DEATH

Soul After Death

(According to Zoroastrianism)

After death the soul goes to the intermediate world (Hamistaken) which corresponds to Purgatory of Christianity The soul of the righteous meets a beautiful maiden, the embodiment of his pure thoughts, pure words and pure actions He crosses safely the bridge of the Judge (Chinavat bridge) which is the seat of judgment and reaches heaven The bridge offers an easy passage for the righteous The Soul passes to 'Amesh—spentas' the golden seat of Ahuramazda

The Soul of the wicked meets a hideous hag, the embodiment of his evil thoughts, evil words and evil actions He fails to cross the bridge and falls into fire or Hell The bridge narrows to the size of the edge of a sword for the wicked

The soul of the dead hovers round the last resting place in the house, for three days It takes its seat near the head and chants the Ushtavaiti Gatha "Happy is he to whom Ahuramazda shall give salvation" Various ceremonies are performed for four days at the spot The Soul has to appear at the Chinavat bridge on the morning of the fourth day In the case of the righteous there is a fragrant wind as it approaches the place and there appears a beautiful young maiden The Soul is quite astonished It asks 'O beautiful maiden! who art thou?' She replies "I am the conscience of your own Self I am an embodiment of your own pure thoughts, pure words and pure actions"

In the case of the unrighteous soul there is a foul-smelling wind when it approaches the bridge and there appears an ugly old hag The soul asks 'Who art thou, O old lady?' She replies "I am the conscience of your own Self I am an embodiment of your own evil thoughts, evil words and evil actions"

What does the Gita say on This

The Blessed Lord said "Many births have been left behind by Me and by thee, O Arjuna, I know them all, but thou knowest not thine, O Parantapa

"This eternal individual Jiva, the world of Jivas, is a ray of myself and at the time of leaving the body, he draws round himself the various senses, that is, the sense of hearing, sense of sight, sense of touch, sense of smell and sense of taste, with the mind as the sixth sense, all these having their abode in Prakriti i e, the world of matter, as distinguished from the Purusha, who is the Paramatman When He acquires a body, and when He departs from the same, the Ishwara takes these and goes out, even as the wind is laden with fragrance gathered from flowers and other sources Verily, the perverted and the deluded do not perceive Him, who thus leaves the body or who resided and enjoyed in the body in conjunction with the senses but the Sages, endowed with the eye of wisdom, do perceive Him

"There are two classes of beings in the world, the perishable and the imperishable The perishable comprises the whole of Creation, together with the Universe of changing forms, whereas the imperishable is the eternal and the immutable Different even from these two is yet the highest spirit known as the Paramatma or the Supreme Self, the immutable, who penetrates and nourishes the three worlds. In so far as I transcend the perishable and the imperishable and because I am superior to them, I am realised as the Purushottama or the highest divinity in the world of Seers and Scriptures

"That time wherein going forth Yogis return not, and also that wherein going forth they return, that time shall I declare to thee, O prince of the Bharatas

"Fire, light, daytime, the bright fortnight, the six months of the northern path, then going forth, the men who know the Eternal go to the Eternal

"Smoke, night time, the dark fortnight, also the six months of the southern path—then the Yogi obtaining the moonlight, returneth

"Light and darkness, these are thought to be the world's everlasting paths, by the one he goeth who returneth not, by the other he who returneth again"

Death and After

Lila said: "Tell me in short, Goddess Saraswati, something more with regard to death, as to whether it is happy or painful to die and what becomes of people after they are dead and gone from here"

The Goddess replied "Dying men are of three sorts and have different results upon their death They are, those who are ignorant, and such as are versed in Yoga, and those that are abstemious and religious"

"Those practising the Dharana Yoga may go wherever they like, after leaving their bodies, and so the reasonable Yogi is at liberty to roam everywhere (It consists in mental meditation and bodily patience and endurance)"

"He who has not practised the Dharana Yoga nor applied himself to acquisition of knowledge, nor has certain reservoir of virtues for the future, is called the ignorant lot and meets with the pains and penalties of death

"He, whose mind is uncontrolled and full of desires and worldly cares and anxieties, becomes as distressed as a lotus torn from its stalk, in fact, it is the subjugation of inordinate passions and destruction of inordinate desires and anxieties, which ensure our true felicity"

"The mind that is not guided by the edicts of the Sastras, nor purified by holiness, but given up to the society of the wicked, is subjected to the burning sensation of fire within himself at the moment of death.

"At the moment when the last gurgling of the throat chokes the breath, the eyesight is dimmed and the countenance fades away, then the Jivatma also becomes hazy in its intellect

"A deep darkness pervades the dimming sight and then starts twinkle before it in day-light The sky appears to be obscured by clouds, and presents a gloomy aspect

"An acute pain traverses the whole frame and a *fata Morgana* dances before the vision; the earth is turned to air and the mid-air seems to be the habitation of the dying person

"The firmament revolves before him, and the tide of the sea seems to bear him away. He is now lifted up in the air, and now hurled down as in a state of dream

"Now he thinks as if he is falling in a dark pit and then as lying in the valley of a hill, he wants to tell aloud his sufferings, but his speech fails him

"He now finds himself as falling down from the sky and now is whirled in the air or wind He is now riding swiftly as in a car, and now finds himself melting as snow

"He desires to acquaint his friends of the torments of life and this world, but he is carried away from them as rapidly as by an aeroplane

"He whirls about as by a rotary machine or turning wheel and is dragged along like a beast by its halter He moves about as in an eddy and is carried around as the machine of some engine

"He is borne in the air as a straw, and is carried about as a cloud by the winds. He soars high like a vapour, and then falls down like a heavy watery cloud pouring out in the sea

"He passes through the endless space and revolves there, to find as it were, a place free from the changes to which the earth and the ocean are subject, (i e a place of peace and rest).

"Thus the rising and falling spirit roves interruptedly, and the soul breathing hard sets the whole body in sore pain and agony

"By degrees, the object of his senses becomes as faint as his failing organs, as the landscape fades to view at the setting of the sun

"He loses the memory of the past and present, is at a loss to know the quarters, after the evening twilight has passed away

"In his fits of fainting, his mind loses its powers of thinking, and he is lost in a state of nescience at the loss of all his thought and sensibility.

"In the state of faintness, the vital breath ceases to circulate through the body; and at the utter stoppage of its circulation, there ensues a collapse much like swooning

"When this state of apoplexy joined with delirium has reached its climax, the body becomes as stiff as stone by the law of inertia, ordained for living beings from the beginning"

Schopenhauer's Views on the 'After-Death State'

Student—Tell me now, in one word, what shall I be after my death? And mind you be clear and precise.

Philosopher—All and nothing.

Student—I thought so I gave you a problem and you solve it by a contradiction That's a very stale trick

Philosopher—Yes, but you raise transcendental questions, and you expect me to answer them in language that is only made of immanent knowledge It's no wonder that a contradiction ensues.

Student—What do you mean by transcendental questions and immanent knowledge? I've heard these expressions before, of course, they are not new to me The professor was fond of using them, but only as predicates of the Deity, and he never talked of anything else, which was all quite right and proper He argued thus If the Deity was in the world itself, he was immanent, if he was somewhere outside it he was transcendent, nothing could be clearer and more obvious You knew where you were But this Kantian rigmarole won't do any more it is antiquated and no longer applicable to modern ideas Why, we've had a whole row of eminent men in the Metropolis of German learning

Philosopher—(aside) German humbug, he means

Student—The mighty Schleiermacher for instance, and that gigantic intellect, Hegel, and at this time of day we've abandoned that nonsense I should rather say we are so far beyond it we can't put up with it any more What's the use of it then? What does it all mean?

Philosopher—Transcendental knowledge is knowledge which passes beyond the bounds of possible experience, and strives to determine the nature of things as they are in themselves. Immanent knowledge on the other hand is knowledge which confines itself entirely within those bounds, so that it cannot apply to anything but actual phenomena As far as you are an individual, death will be the end of you But your individuality is not your true and inmost being, it is only the outward manifestation of it It is not the thing in itself, but only the phenomenon presented in the form of time, and therefore with a beginning and an end But your real being knows neither time nor beginning nor end nor yet the limits of any given individual It is everywhere present in every individual and no individual can exist apart from it So when death comes, on the one hand you are annihilated as an individual, on the other, you are and remain everything That is what I meant when I said that after your death you would be all and nothing It is difficult to find a more precise answer to your question and at the same time be brief The answer is contradictory, I admit, but it is so simply because your life is in time, and the immortal part of you in Eternity. You may put the matter thus· Your immortal part is something that does not last in time and yet is indestructible, but there you have another contradiction You see that by trying to bring the transcendental within the limits of immanent knowledge It is in some sort doing violence to the latter by misusing it for ends it was never meant to serve.

Student—Look here, I shan't give two pence for your immortality unless I'm to remain an individual

Philosopher—Well, perhaps I may be able to satisfy you on this point Suppose I guarantee you that after death you shall remain an individual but only on condition that you first spend three months of complete unconsciousness

Student—I shall have no objection to that

Philosopher—But, remember, if people are completely unconscious, they take no account of time So, when you are dead, it's all the same to you whether three months pass in the world of unconsciousness, or ten thousand years In one case as in the other, it is simply a matter of believing what is told you, when awake So far then you can afford to be indifferent whether it is three months or ten thousand years that pass before you recover your individuality

Student—Yes, if it comes to that, I suppose you are right

Philosopher—And if by chance, after those ten thousand years gone by, no one ever thinks of awakening you, I fancy it would be a great misfortune You would have become quite accustomed to non-existence after so long a spell of it—following upon such a very few years of life At any rate you may be sure you would be perfectly ignorant of the whole thing. Further, if you knew that the mysterious power which keeps you in your present state of life had never once ceased in those ten thousand years to bring forth other phenomena like yourself, and to endow them with life, it would fully console you

Student—Indeed' so you think that you're quietly going to do me out of my individuality with all this fine talk But I'm open to your tricks I tell you I won't exist unless I can have my individuality, I'm not going to put off with 'mysterious powers, and what you call 'phenomena' I can't do without my individuality, and I won't give it up

Philosopher—You mean, I suppose, that your individuality is such a delightful thing—so splendid, so perfect, and beyond comparison—that you can't imagine anything better. Aren't you ready to exchange your present state for one which if we can judge by what is told us, may possibly be superior and more endurable.

Student—Don't you see that my individuality be it what it may, is my very self? To me it is the most important thing in the world

"For God is God and I am I"

I want to exist, I, I That's the main thing I don't care about existence which has to be proved to be mine before I can believe it

Philosopher—Think what you're doing' When you say I, I I want to exist, is it not you alone that say this Everything says it, absolutely everything that has the faintest trace of consciousness It follows then, that this desire of yours is just the part of you that is not individual—the part that is common to all things without distinction It is the cry not of the individual, but of existence itself, it is the intrinsic element in everything that exists, nay, it is the cause of anything existing at all This desire craves for and so is satisfied with nothing less than existence in general—not any definite individual existence. No! that is not its aim. It sems to be so only because this desire will attain consciousness only in the individual, and therefore looks as though it were concerned with nothing but the individual. There lies the illusion, an illusion it is true, in which the individual is held fast; but if he reflects, he can break the fetters and set himself free. It is only indirectly, I say, that the individual has this violent craving for existence. It is the will to live which is the real and direct aspirant—alike and identical in all things. Since then, existence is the free work, nay, the mere reflection of the will, where existence, is, there too must be a will; and for the moment, the will finds its satisfaction in existence itself, so far, I mean, as that which never rests, but presses forward eternally, can ever find any satisfaction at all. The will is careless of the individual, the individual is not its business; although as I have said, this seems to be the case, because the individual has no direct consciousness of will except in himself. The effect of this is to make the individual careful to maintain his own existence, and if this were not so, there would be no surety of preservation of the species. From all this it is clear that individuality is not a form of perfection, but rather of limitation, and so to be freed from it is not loss but gain. Trouble yourself no more about the matter. Once thoroughly recognize what you are, what your existence really is, namely, the universal will, to live and the whole question will seem to you childish and most ridiculous.

Student—You are childish yourself and most ridiculous, like all philosophers, and as a man of my age lets himself in for a quarter of an hour's talk with such fools, it is only because it amuses me and passes the time I've more important business to attend to, so Good-bye!

Last Thought Forms

The last thought of a man governs his future destiny The last thought of a man determines his future birth. Lord Krishna says in Bhagavad Gita. "Whosoever at the end abandoneth the body, thinking upon any being, to that being only he goeth, O Kaunteya, ever to that conformed in nature". (Chap. VIII, 6)

Ajamila lost his pious conduct, and led a detestable living He fell into evil depth of sinful habits and resorted to theft and robbery He became a slave of a public woman He became the father of ten children, the last of whom was called Narayana

When he was about to die, he was absorbed in the thoughts of his last son Three fearful messengers of death advanced towards Ajamila Ajamila cried aloud in great distress the last son's name "Narayana"

On a mere mention of the name of "Narayana", the attendants of Lord Hari came speedily along and obstructed the messengers of death They took him to Vaikuntha or the world of Vishnu

The Soul of Sisupala entered the Supreme Lord with an effulgent spark of ineffable glory and mag nificence This vile Sisupala spent his lifetime in reviling Lord Krishna and then he entered the Lord.

The worm on the wall when stung by the wasp changes into the form of the latter Similarly the man who focuses his hate on Lord Krishna gets rid of his sins and reaches that Lord by regular devotion, as the Gopis did by Kama (passion), Kamsa by fear, Sisupala by hatred and Narada by love

Lord Krishna says in Gita "Whoever constantly thinks of me intensely and with one-pointed mind, to such steadfast Yogis, I am easily attainable, and having thus reached Me and merged in Me, they are not born again in the fleeting world of woe and misery. Oh Arjuna' While all the worlds, created by Brahma, are limited by time and have their moment of dissolution, on reaching Me, there is no rebirth, therefore at all times, meditate on Me, the Supreme Vasudeva and with mind and intellect fixed on Me Doubtless you will attain me"

(Chapter VIII—14, 15, 16)

This constant practice of fixing the mind on the Lord, although a man is engaged in worldly pursuits, will enable him to intuitively and automatically think of the Lord, even at the time of his departure The Lord says: "With the mind thus engaged in the Yoga of constant practice, not deflected by any other obstacles, one attains the Supreme Purusha of resplendent glory The Lord further says, "At the time of death, he who thinks of My real Being as the Supreme Lord Sri Krishna or Narayana, leaves the body and verily reaches my Being Doubt this not! In whatever form a man thinks of Me at the time of death, that form he attains, that form again being the result of nourishing that thought in a particular groove and by constant meditation of the same"

The Lord further says "He who further establishes his mind on Me, even at the time of forthgoing and who is in that Divine state of renouncing everything and of dwelling in Brahman or Brahmic state, is free from delusion."

(B G II—72)

He who has a strong habit of using snuff in his life imitates the act of snuffing with his fingers when he is in an unconscious state just before his death. So strong is the habit of snuffing in this man

The last thought of a licentious man will be the thought of his woman The last thought of an inveterate drunkard will be that of his peg of liquor The last thought of a greedy money-lender will be that of his money The last thought of a fighting soldier will be that of shooting his enemy The last thought of a mother who is intensely attached to her only son will be that of her son only

Raja Bharata nursed a deer out of mercy and became attached to it His last thought was the thought of that deer Hence he had to take the birth of a deer, but he had memory of his last birth as he was an advanced Soul.

The last thought will be the thought of God only for that man who has disciplined his mind all throughout his life and who has tried to fix the mind on the Lord through constant practice It cannot come by a stray practice in a day or two in a week or a month. It is a lifelong endeavour and struggle.

Personality and Individuality

There is a distinction between personality and individuality Many have no clear understanding of these two terms. They get these mixed up and are confused Some people think that personality is individuality and individuality is personality That which distinguishes a person from a thing or one person from another is personality Personality in common parlance refers to the body When a man is tall, has good complexion and beautiful features, when his face has a fine cut, we say that Mr So-and-so has a charming personality When one is able to influence others, people say that such-and-such a man has a strong personality When one is timid and shy we say that such-and-such a man has weak personality, he must develop his personality Personality counts much in society for success in life

The term personality comes from the Latin persona, the mask Personality is that particular consciousness which concerns the physical body Mr or Mrs or Miss So-and-so is the personality Hunger, thirst, physical beauty, black or red colour, height, stature, anger and all the limitations of the body relate to the personality He is a Brahmin He is a Sannyasi He is a merchant He is a doctor. All these concern the personality. This is the mask which the man is putting on now

Death destroys the personality but it cannot annihilate the individuality. Individuality is separate and has distinct existence It is something which is beyond the body. It has no relation to your personality at all. It is the sense of 'I'. It is like a continuous current. It is the continuity of the one thought, the thought of 'I' All other thoughts are centred round this 'I' I was a body I became a man I was a doctor I ate I drank I spoke I meditated I talked I went to America, England, France and Germany The same 'I' has gone through all these experiences 'I' is the dweller in this body 'I' is the same in childhood, youth and old age.

Personality changes but your individuality, the sense of 'I' can never change because the sense of 'I' will continue to exist with you After leaving this physical body the sense of 'I' continues to exist After death you take the sense of 'I' with you Even in dream you have the sense of 'I' within Even in deep sleep you have the sense of 'I' If you have not got the sense of 'I' in deep sleep you would not remember that you slept happily

You can lose this individuality by becoming one with the supreme self or Para Brahman through meditation and Nirvikalpa Samadhi Just as the water in the pot becomes one with the ocean when the pot is broken, so also the individuality becomes one with the Infinity or the Universality when ignorance is destroyed, when the idea of separateness is annihilated through knowledge of the Imperishable or Brahma Jnana Do you see now clearly the difference between personality and individuality?

Belief of the Ancient Egyptians

The Egyptians believed in a 'double' which was like a shadow of the body This double remained as long as the body remained. The Soul was only a double. It had no individuality of its own. It was never able to do away with its connection with the body If the body was injured in any part the double or Soul was also injured Hence they preserved the bodies to keep the soul intact They took recourse to mummification of the bodies of the dead They wanted to preserve the dead bodies for a very long time in order to make the departed Soul immortal

The double remained only so long as the body remained. If the corpse is destroyed, the departed Soul also must perish The Soul after death wandered about freely all over the world, and returned to the place where the corpse was kept with intense thirst and hunger

The Chaldeans also believed in a double which would be destroyed if the body were destroyed. They expected a resurrection of the corpse again to life They could not conceive of a state without this physical body

The ancient Egyptians or Chaldeans could never entirely dissociate the idea of the Soul from the corpse of the departed or the place of burial Some of the Christians expect a resurrection of the corpse Hence they embalm and bury the dead They do not cremate the dead bodies, just as the Hindus do They still believe that the body will rise after death

The Hindus do not wish that departed Souls should hover round the body even for a minute

The departed Soul is always extremely desirous to enjoy life once more It wishes to enter a physical body to fulfil its desires The Hindus do not wish that the Souls be earth-bound They wish that the Souls should march quickly towards their abode of happiness That is the reason why they cremate the dead bodies at once.

CHAPTER FIVE

DOCTRINE OF REINCARNATION

Doctrine of Reincarnation

Emerson, Plato, Pythagoras had perfect belief in the doctrine of reincarnation. The doctrine of reincarnation is the foundation of Hinduism and Buddhism The ancient Egyptians believed it The Greek philosophers made it the corner-stone of their philosophy

Man clings to this earthly life This clinging to life proves that there is past experience and existence This proves also that there is a future life. Man likes this life immensely and strongly yearns for a future life also

Some are born and pass out within a few weeks, a few months, a few years Some children die in the womb Some are centenarians Why is this? Why do some people come and live for a short time and others live longer? Is this accidental? Is there any law that governs life and death? Do the human beings come here and pass out without any definite purpose? There is a law which governs life and death That law is the law of cause and effect

The law of cause and effect governs everything. The law of cause and effect is inexorable and all-powerful This whole world runs under this supreme law All the other laws come under this law The law of Karma is the law of cause and effect God does not punish any one Man reaps the fruits of his Karma The law of cause and effect operates on him He reaps a harvest of pleasure for his good actions He suffers and experiences pain and disease, loss of property for his wicked actions

Instinct is the result of past experience One of the important arguments for reincarnation has been built on this by the Hindus. The past experiences of death remain in the subconscious mind or Chitta in a latent or dormant state They are in the form of Samskaras or impressions They are working underneath the conscious, objective mind Man is terribly afraid of death, because the past experience of pain is in the subconscious mind

Love at first sight is a certain feeling of a previous life lived together. These Souls loved before They remember that and actually feel as if they had met each other Such loves are not at all a matter of sex, and are seldom broken off Lord Buddha told his wife of her kindness to him in a previous birth and several times gave details of the previous lives of other people

Every effect must have a cause Something cannot come out of nothing. Existence cannot come out of non-existence This is the fundamental principle of modern science This is the fundamental doctrine of philosophy also You have not come out of nothing There is a cause for your existence here One is born blind One is a genius, One is dull One is rich One is poor One is healthy One is sickly There is a definite cause for all these things

The cause is the unmanifested condition of the effect The effect is the manifested state of the cause Tree is the cause The seed is the effect Vapour is the cause Rain is the effect The whole tree remains in the seed in a potential form The whole human form remains in the drop of semen in an invisible potential state The seed of a banyan tree can produce only a banyan tree but not a mango tree The drop of human semen can produce only a human being but not a horse From a tiny drop of semen a big human form with various limbs and organs comes out What a great marvel ! From a small seed a gigantic banyan tree comes out What a great wonder ! Just close your eyes and reflect over this mystery You will be struck with awe and wonder

Within the gross physical body there is another subtle body or Linga Sareera or Sukshma Deha. This subtle body comes out with all its impressions and tendencies at the time of death of the gross physical body It is like vapour It cannot be seen by the naked eye It is the subtle body that goes to heaven. It manifests again in a gross form. This remanifestation of the subtle form into the gross physical form is called the law of reincarnation . You may deny this law, but the law is there It is inexorable and unrelenting If you deny the law, it clearly shows that you are quite ignorant of it and it will surely operate whether you admit it or not The light of the sun is there whether the owl accepts it or not

You acquire your knowledge through experiences. A man plays on the harmonium. He places each finger on each key consciously He repeats it again and again After some time the movement of the fingers becomes a habit He plays a tune without looking into the particular keys Even so your tendencies are the result of your past conscious actions

Sri Sankara and Sri Jnana Dev knew the Vedas and other Shastras in their boyhood A child plays on the piano in a masterly manner. A child delivers lectures on Gita. Goethe, the eminent German poet, was the master of seventeen languages These geniuses did not acquire these in this life They must have had them in past lives

Every child is born with certain tendencies or predilections generated by past conscious actions No child is born with a vacant mind or a clean blank page of a mind, a *tabula rasa*. We have had past lives This is the emphatic declaration of the great sages Rishis and Yogis of the past and of modern times Jesus Christ believed in it He says in the Bible "Before Abraham was, I am" Reincarnation made its appearance in the early Christian Church Elijah is reborn as John the Baptist

Heredity cannot explain all these inequalities and diversities the cases of geniuses The parents, brothers and sisters of these prodigies are quite common persons Tendencies are the result of the past actions They do not come through heredity The geniuses have gained their talents in their previous lives

If your desires are not gratified in this life under present conditions, you will have to come back again to this earth-plane for their fulfilment If you have a strong desire to become a Master Musician in this birth and if you cannot achieve this and still cherish this desire, this desire will bring you back to this earth-plane and place you in suitable environments and favourable conditions You will start again from your childhood with a tendency to become a Master Musician

An objection is brought against the doctrine of reincarnation That objection is "Why do we not remember our past?" Do you remember what you did in your childhood? Will you say you did not exist then, because you cannot remember? Certainly not. If your existence depends upon your memory then this argument proves that you did not exist as children, because you do not remember your childhood The details have passed out of your memory, but the knowledge you have acquired through your experience is part and parcel of your being Those experiences are still in your subconscious mind or Chitta as impressions

If you remember your past you may make a bad use of the present Your inveterate enemy in your past life may be born as your son in this life If you remember the past you will draw your sword to kill him Feelings of enmity will rise in your heart at once When you enter college you carry with you all the knowledge you acquired at school You increase and develop that kind of knowledge in your higher studies You do not remember fully everything you did at schools, yet the experience is there when you are in the college Even so past experience influences your present life

Mother Nature has concealed the past from you It is not desirable to remember the past Suppose for a moment you know the past—you know that you have committed a sinful action in your past life and you are going to suffer for it You will be thinking of this always You will worry yourself constantly You will not have sound sleep You will not relish your food That is the reason why sages tell you "Do not think of the past Do not plan for the future Mould your present Live in the solid present Entertain good thoughts Do virtuous actions" You can make your future better

A Yogi can remember his past lives, through concentration on the Samskaras He can tell you all about your past lives also through concentration on the Samskaras or impressions that are lodged in your subconscious mind

Your present birth is the result of your past actions All the actions that you do now will determine your future birth You have set the law of causation in motion and you are caught in this wheel of birth and death This is the law of reincarnation This law binds all beings When you attain the perfect knowledge of the Imperishable the wheel is broken and you attain freedom and perfection

Your experiences can hardly be destroyed Your actions are endowed with an invisible power called Adrishtam or Apurva which produce fruits The actions manifest again as tendencies If you do several merciful acts you develop a very strong tendency to do acts of mercy Those who are merciful in this birth have done great acts of mercy in their previous births

Reincarnation depends upon Karma If a man does actions of a beastly nature he will take the birth of an animal

The doctrine of reincarnation is as old as the Vedas or the Himalayas The doctrine of reincarnation will solve many problems of life Each word, thought and deed lays up a store for you Be good Do good Entertain good thoughts Do virtuous actions Purify your heart Meditate regularly on the Immortal Atman, thy universal Self. You will free yourself from the round of births and deaths and attain Immortality and Eternal Bliss in this very life

Karma and Reincarnation (ii)

The doctrine of reincarnation is accepted by the majority of mankind at the present day It has been held as true by the mightiest Eastern nations The ancient civilisation of Egypt was built upon this doctrine and it was handed over to Pythagoras, Plato, Virgil and Ovid, who scattered it through Greece and Italy It was the key-note of Plato's philosophy when he says that all knowledge is reminiscence It was wholly adopted by the Neo-Platonists like Plotinus and Proclas The hundreds of millions of Hindus, Buddhists and Jains have made that doctrine the foundation of their philosophy, religion, government and social institutions It was a cardinal point in the religion of the Persian Unagi The doctrine of Metempsychosis was an essential principle of the Druid faith and was impressed upon the Celts, the Gauls and the Britons Among the Arabs' philosophers it was a favourite idea The rites and ceremonies of Romans, Druids and Hebrews expressed this truth forcibly The Jains adopted it after the Babylonian captivity John the Baptist was to them a second Elijah Jesus was thought to be a reappearance of John the Baptist or one of the old prophets The Roman Catholic purgatory seems to be a makeshift contrived to take its place Philosophers like Kant Schelling and Schopenhauer have upheld this doctrine Theologians like Julius Muller, Dorner and Edward Beecher have maintained it And today it reigns over the Burmese Siamese, Chinese, Japanese, Tartarian Tibetian, East Indian and Ceylonese including at least 750 millions mankind and nearly two-thirds of the human race Is it not surprising then that this great and grand philosophical education which the Hindus and Buddhists and Jains gave to the world centuries and centuries before the Christian Era should or could be blotted out of existence from the Western and European world by the soul blighting and absurd dogmas of the dark ages that supervened? By the persecution of the wise men and destruction of the innumerable works in the library of Constantinople, the Church hierarchy managed to plunge the whole of Europe into mental darkness which has given the world the black record of inquisition and the loss of millions of human lives through religious wars and persecutions

Here is a challenge to the non-believers of the Hindu theory of transmigration In Delhi recently the little girl Santi Devi gave a vivid description of her past life There was great sensation in Delhi and Muttra, nay, throughout the United Provinces There was a great assembly of persons to hear her statements She recognised her husband and child of her previous birth who are living in Muttra She pointed out the place where money was kept and an old well in the house which is covered now All her statements were duly verified and corroborated by respectable eye-witnesses Several cases like this have occurred in Rangoon, Sitapur and various other places They are quite common now In such cases the Jiva takes immediate rebirth with the old astral body or Linga Sarira That is the reason why memory of previous birth comes in He did not stay in the mental world for a long time to rebuild a new mind and astral body according to his various experiences of the world.

Transmigration made its appearance in the early Christian church Elijah was reborn as John the Baptist "Did the blind man sin, or his parents that he was born blind?" ask the believers in transmitted retribution There is a period of anxiety immediately after death when angels contend with demons for the possession of the departing soul on its way to purgatory

Pythagoras and others have got their belief in metempsychosis from India only Pythagoras who flourished in the 6th century also taught a doctrine of transmigration, and, curiously enough, prescribed abstinence from the eating of flesh

The suckling of a child and the act of swimming of a duckling—these instinctive acts are proofs of memory which must be the result of their corresponding and inseparable impressions left by the same acts in a previous incarnation, never mind when and where Every act leaves Samskaras in the Chitta which causes memory Memory in its own turn leads to fresh actions and fresh impressions This cycle or Chakrika goes on from eternity like the analogy of seed and tree

There is no beginning for them, the desire to live being eternal, for them, i e, for the desires Desires have no beginning or end every being is clinging to this physical life (Abhinivesa) This "will to live" is eternal Experiences are also without beginning You cannot think of a time when this feeling of 'Aham' or 'I' has not existed This 'I' exists continuously without any interruption From this we can very easily infer that there have been previous births for us

Now could there be fear of death to avoid pain, in any being who has only been born, if he has no experience of liability to death, it being understood that desire to avoid anything is only caused by remembrance suffered in consequence thereof Nothing which is inherent in anything stands in need of a cause How should it be that a child, who has not experienced this liability to death in the present life, should, as he may be falling away from the mother's lap, begin to tremble and hold with his hands tightly the necklace hanging on her breast? How is it that such a child should experience the fear of death, which can only be caused by the memory of the pain consequent upon aversion to death, whose existence is inferred by the trembling of the child?

We have got boy-geniuses A boy of five becomes an expert in piano or violin Sri Jnanadev wrote his commentary "Jnaneshwari" on the Gita when he was fourteen years old There had been boy-mathematicians There was the boy Bhagavatar in Madras who conducted Kathas when he was eight years old How could you explain this strange phenomenon? This is not a freak of nature The theory of transmigration only could explain all these things If one man gets deep grooves in his mind by learning music or mathematics in this birth he carries these impressions to the next birth and becomes a prodigy in these sciences even when he is a boy

According to the Christian faith, the ultimate fate of the righteous is life eternal, of the evil, everlasting fire or eternal damnation How could this be? No opportunity is afforded to the sinner to purify himself in later births

The doctrine of reincarnation is common to Hinduism, Buddhism and Jainism What is reincarnation? Reincarnation is the doctrine that souls enter this life not as fresh creations, but a long course of previous existences has to be passed through before they reach final destination What possible motion in the brain causes the idea 'I am I'? This recognition of a real unit does not vary from the cradle to the grave From childhood to old age, during the whole course of the total change of all brain-molecules, 'I am I' is undisturbed This 'I am I' is the soul It is this soul which makes memory possible It has its own consciousness and not the consciousness of anyone else Therefore it is a unit existing by itself The law of the conservation of energy is true in the physical as well as in the spiritual world. Therefore as no atom can be created or destroyed, so also no soul-entity can be created or destroyed What becomes of soul then after what we call death? No power in the universe can annihilate it

Reincarnation is the only doctrine which gives a complete solution of the much-disputed question of original sin There cannot be greater injustice in the world than the fact that I am suffering for the transgression of my ancestor Adonis responsibility for our sin is only a make-shift of the theologians No one but the individual himself can be blamed for his wrong doing Are not the courts of law of the United States founded on the ideas of Justice? Will any judge sitting on the throne of justice be justified in accepting the death—the voluntary suicide of Mr B as the proper retribution for the murder committed by Mr A? And if he does that, will not the same judge be arraigned before a superior court having knowingly abetted the suicide of B? And still we are asked to believe that the guilt of one man can be washed by the suffering of another

But the doctrine of reincarnation assists most when we look at the inequality and injustice and evil in the world and seek for the solution Why is one man born rich and the other poor? Why is one man born in Central Africa among the cannibals and the other in the peaceful part of India? Why was King George born to rule over the territories on which the sun never set and why is a labourer in Assam to work as a slave in an Englishman's tea garden? What is the cause for this apparent injustice? Even those who have belief in the personal creator of the universe must believe in this doctrine of reincarnation in order to exonerate God from the charge of maliciousness

Even in the New Testament there is sufficient evidence for reincarnation In St John IX—2, a question is put to Jesus by his disciples—Which did sin this man or his parents that he was born blind? This refers to two popular theories of the time—one that of Moses who taught that the sin of fathers would descend on children to the third and the fourth generation, and the other, that of the doctrine of reincarnation Jesus merely says that neither that man's sin nor his father's sin was the cause of his blindness, he does not deny the pre-existence of that man Lord Jesus also means that John took the reincarnation of Elijah

But people may say—if this doctrine is true, how is it that he does not remember his past reincarnation? I will ask such people in what way do we exercise the faculty of memory? Certainly so far as we are living in a body we exercise it through the brain In passing from one incarnation to the other, the soul does not carry the former brain in the new body Even during the course of one life, do we always remember our past doings? Can any one remember that wonderful epoch—the infancy?

If you have a knowledge of the Raja Yogic technique of perceiving the impressions directly through the Raja Yogic Samyama (Dharana Dhyana and Samadhi at one time) you can remember your past lives In Raja Yoga philosophy of Patanjali Maharshi, you will find "Samskara-Sakshat-Karanat Purvajati Jnanam" "By perceiving the impressions, comes the knowledge of past life" Ch III—18 All experiences that you have had in various births remain in the form of impressions or residual potencies in Chitta or subconscious mind They remain in a very, very subtle form, just as the sound remains in a subtle state in the gramophone record These impressions assume the forms of waves and you get memory of past experiences Therefore if the Yogi can make a Samyama on these past experiences, in the Chitta he can remember all the details of all his past lives

Reincarnation is Quite True (1)

Man can hardly attain perfection in one life He has to develop his heart, intellect and hand He has to mould his character in a perfect manner He has to develop various virtuous qualities such as mercy, tolerance, love, forgiveness, equal vision, courage, etc He has to learn many lessons and experiences in this great world-school Therefore he has to take many lives Reincarnation is very true One small life is a part of the long series that stretches behind you and in front of you It is quite insignificant One gains a little experience only He evolves very little During the course of one life man does many evil actions He does very little goond actions Very few die as good men Christians believe that one life determines and settles everything. How could this be? How can the everlasting future of man be made to depend on that one small, little insignificant life? If in that life he believes in Christ, he will get eternal peace in heaven. if he is an unbeliever in that life, he will get eternal damnation, he will be thrown for ever in the lake of fire or horrible hell Is this not the most irrational doctrine? Should he not get his chances for correction and improvement? The doctrine of reincarnation is quite rational It gives ample chances for man's rectification, growth and gradual evolution

Transmigration of Souls

The word "transmigration" means passing from one life to another The one great and fundamental tenet of most schools of Indian Philosophy, with the exception of the Charvaka or the materialist, is the belief in the immortality of the Soul The Soul passes through a number of lives for attaining perfection This is technically called "Transmigration of Souls'

Belief in the Metempsychosis or transmigration of Soul dates from primeval times It is as early as primitive man One solution of the mystery of death and a consoling thought about death is the indestructibility of the Soul and its existence after death in other forms. In India the ancient Aryans found in it the solution of the age-long problem of human suffering and developed it into a very distinct religious doctrine

The purpose of transmigration is not reward or punishment, but betterment and perfection It prepares the human being for the ultimate realisation which frees him from the cycle of births and deaths It is not possible to achieve perfection and absolute freedom without a plurality of lives

Man develops tendency and aptitude in several births and becomes a genius in one birth Buddha gained experiences in several births. He became a Buddha only in his last birth In one birth all virtues cannot be developed One can cultivate the virtues by gradual evolution The baby sucks, the young duck swims Who taught this? They are the Samskaras or the tendencies of previous births

There had been many instances of children like Santi Devi, etc who have narrated all about their previous lives All these have been fully corroborated also The children have actually pointed out their houses in which they lived in their previous life

Soul, retribution, transmigration, divinity were all accepted by Plato Pythagoras also taught the doctrine of transmigration Buddha also taught the doctrine of transmigration

The older Egyptians embalmed their dead and buried them in the best tombs they could afford The deceased had a kind of twin Soul, one half of which remained in the tomb as long as the body continued undecayed, while the other proceeded on passport to the immortal Gods The requisite indication was given by a divine Judge, whose opinion as to destiny was final Transmigration in some obscure form was nevertheless held by the Egyptian priesthood

The human body is only a vesture and dwelling place for the immortal Soul The Soul can certainly re-inhabit another dwelling place and put on another vesture in order to develop and realise better than before the Divine plan and purpose for it The Creator has so planned. The Soul of a depraved and corrupted human being is given another training in another body The evolution of all beings is for a better condition Evolution to the higher and not deterioration to the lower is generally the law and principle of Nature But there is exception to the general rule

The Soul armed with the little virtue and divinity gained in the previous existence enters another life to increase, develop and better that original stock There is now a greater response of the body controlled by the Soul to God, Goodness, Truth, Holiness and other attributes of God

No opportunity is afforded to the sinner to purify himself in later births His finite sin, if not somehow purged, precipitates him at death into endless misery This cannot be This is not reasonable. The doctrine of transmigration gives ample scope for the sinner to correct and educate himself in the future births Vedanta says that there is hope of salvation even for the worst sinner

He reaps the harvest of his misdeeds for a limited period After he has been purged of his sins, he is again born as a rational being and is thus given a fresh chance for working out his emancipation with freedom of will to choose the right path or the wrong one, and with knowledge to distinguish the one from the other

You are responsible for your well-being or otherwise, through your own Karma or action. The diversity in individual characters, the different predilections or tendencies of the different children at their births and the inequalities of human lives can only be accounted for and explained through the Law of Karma The Law of Karma gives liberty and freedom to an individual to grow to his full perfection

The image of a man is reflected in a mirror Nothing passes from the man to the image The image is not the same as the man nor yet is it another In exactly the same way rebirth takes place The new being is like the image The Karma which gives rise to the new being is like the mirror, through the agency of which the image of the man is reflected

The enlightening influences of Yogis and Sages, their lives and teachings assert themselves more and more in the new life The light of God is more sought after and the gravitation towards God becomes stronger and stronger More and more the life gets fitted to see God and hear His voice Progress advances from one existence to the next—we cannot say through how many lives—until the final and stainless state of perfection is reached and the individual Soul merges itself in the Supreme Soul.

Whence have I come? Whither shall I go? These questions will be asked by every intelligent person They are problems of life Your present life is but one in a series of countless incarnations, though not all in the human form necessarily

The union of the Soul with a particular body is known as birth and its separation therefrom is called death When the Soul leaves its physical sheath, it transmigrates into another body, human, animal or even vegetable, according to its merits The Kathopanishad says "Now I will tell you, O Nachiketas, the eternal and divine mystery as to how the Soul fares after attaining death. Some Souls attain to other bodies, while some fall to the vegetable state according to their action and knowledge" 1-2-18

The process of transmigration continues till the Soul, being purged of all its impurities and having acquired a true and full knowledge of the Imperishable Soul by Yoga attains Mukti or the final emancipation and enjoys perfect eternal bliss by its union with the Supreme Self or Para Brahman

According to Indian philosophy there is a subtle body or Sukshma Sareera within the physical body When the physical body perishes, this subtle body does not perish It moves to heaven to enjoy the fruits of its good actions done here This subtle body perishes only when the Soul attains the final emancipation The impressions or Samskaras, Vasanas or the tendencies, are carried in the subtle body.

There are blessed Souls like Vama Dev, Jnana Dev, Dattatreya, Ashtavakra and Sankaracharya, who in their very first entry into the world may attain a high degree of perfection before death They are all born Siddhas There are some other Souls who will need few further rebirths for their full perfection and attainment of Moksha

A good Soul makes a good body. a bad Soul a bad body Body is an indispensable aid to the Soul in its progress towards God The body was designed by God to carry the Soul in its onward march Petrol and steam are great forces But by themselves they cannot make the journey with a definite course and a definite destination They must be harnessed to a machine, a running train or steamer. A pilot or a driver puts petrol or steam into the conveyance and drives and steers it towards his destination Therefore the Soul must have a body to run its course and reach its destination in God.

When knowledge of the Imperishable is attained, there is no more transmigration Mother Prakriti's work is over now She shows all the experiences of this world to the individual Soul and takes him higher and higher through various bodies till he regains back his essential divine nature, till he merges himself in the Supreme Self or Para Brahman

Strive by every means to make your life better by ceaseless spiritual culture and practical Yoga Sadhana. Only by enlightenment or Brahma Jnana you can obtain deliverance from the wearisome round of births and deaths

Theory of Rebirth

Man can be compared to a plant. He grows and flourishes like a plant and dies in the end but not completely The plant also grows and flourishes and dies in the end. It leaves behind it the seed which produces a new plant. Man leaves when dying his Karma behind,—the good and bad actions of his life The physical body may die and disintegrate, but the impressions of his actions do not die He has to take birth again to enjoy the fruits of these actions No life can be the first, for it is the fruit of previous actions, nor the last. for its actions must be expiated in the next life following Therefore, Samsara or phenomenal existence is without beginning and end But there is no Samsara for a Jivanmukta or liberated sage who is resting in his own Sat-Chit-Ananda Swaroopa.

When a man dies he carries with him the permanent Linga Sareera, which is made up of 5 Jnana

Indriyas, 5 Karma Indriyas, 5 Pranas, mind, Buddhi, Chitta and Ahamkara and the changing Karmasraya (receptacle of works), the actions of the Soul, which determines the formation of the next life

Sri Jnana Dev, late reputed Yogi of Alandi, wrote his commentary on Gita Jnaneshwari when he was only sixteen years old He was a born Siddha You can also become a Siddha if you try in right earnest What one has attained can be achieved by another also

If a new-born child who has not done any wrong action in this birth undergoes great suffering, this is the fruit of some evil deed done in the previous birth If you ask, how the person was induced to do a wrong action in his former birth, the answer is that it was the result of some wrong action done in a birth still anterior and so on

Many intelligent fathers have sons with dull intellect If a shepherd boy gave you some food and water in your previous birth when you were dying of starvation, he will be born in this birth as your son, with a dull intellect to enjoy your property.

When creatures are born, they evince a desire to suck the breast and show an instinct of terror Therefore it follows that they remember the sucking of the breast and the pains experienced in the previous birth This shows that there is rebirth

Even a child exhibits Harsha (exhilaration), Soka (grief), fear, anger, pleasure and pain. The Dharmadharma Samskaras of this birth cannot be the cause of these. The Samskaras of the previous birth must have a support (Asraya) From this we can clearly infer the existence of Jiva in the previous birth, and the Jiva is Anadi or beginningless If you do not accept that the Jiva is Anadi, the two Doshas viz, Kritanasa and Akritabhyagama will creep in Pleasure and pain which are the fruits of virtuous and vicious actions done previously will pass away without being enjoyed This is the Dosha of Kritanasa. So also, one will have to enjoy the pleasure and pain, the fruits of good and evil actions, which were done by him previously This is the Dosha of Akritabhyagama In order to get rid of these two Doshas, we will have to accept that the Jiva is Anadi or beginningless

Some Yogic students ask me "How long should one practise Sirshasana or Paschimottanasana or Kumbhak or Mahamudra to awaken Kundalini? Nothing is mentioned on this point in any book on Yoga" A student starts his Sadhana from the point or stage he left in his previous birth That is the reason why Lord Krishna says to Arjuna "Or he may be born in a family of wise Yogins There he recovereth the characteristics belonging to his former body and with these he again laboureth for perfection, O Joy of the Kurus" Chap VI-42, 43 It all depends upon the degree of purity stage of evolution, the degree of purification of Nadis and the Pranayama Kosha, degree of Vairagya and yearning for liberation

Some are born with purity and other requisites of realisation on account of their having undergone the necessary discipline in their past life They are born Siddhas Guru Nanak, Jnana Dev of Alandi, Vama Dev, Ashtavakra, were all adepts from their very boyhood Guru Nanak asked his teacher in the school when he was a boy, about the significance of OM Vama Dev delivered lectures on Vedanta when he was dwelling in his mother's womb

Man does actions with the expectation of getting fruits and so he takes a birth to enjoy the fruits of his actions In the next birth, he does some more actions and he has to take another birth In this manner the Samsaric wheel is revolving from eternity to eternity When one gets knowledge of the Self, he is liberated from this round of births and deaths. Karma is beginningless and Samsara is also beginningless When a man does actions without expectation of fruits in selfless spirit all the fetters of Karma get loosened gradually

Die to live Kill this little 'I' and attain immortality Live in Brahman You will live for ever Passess Atman You will have eternal life Identify with your soul You will cross the ocean of death or Samsara Rest in your Satchidananda Swaroopa You will have everlasting life

A leech moves on a blade of grass and reaches the end of the blade It first catches hold of another blade with the fore-part of its body and then draws its hind part on to it Even so, the Jivatman (individual soul) abandons the present body at the time of death, fashions the future body by his thought and then enters into that body.

A good or bad deed always brings its good or bad fruits You will find in Mahabharata. "Just as a calf finds out its mother among a thousand cows, so also an action that was performed in a previous birth follows the doer"

Yadrisham kriyate karma tadrisham
bhujyate phalam
Yadrisham vapyate bijam tadrisham
prapyate phalam

Just as the fruit corresponds to the seed that has been sown, so also the fruit of the actions that are performed by us correspond to the nature of the actions that we perform This is an infallible law of nature He who has sown the seed of a mango tree cannot expect a jack fruit He who has done evil actions throughout his life, cannot expect happiness, peace and prosperity in his next life

"Many are the times we have all been together in the past, and also been separated and so again shall it be in the future Even as a heap of grain removed from granary to granary ever assumes new order of arrangement and new combination, so is the case with Jiva (human beings) in the universe through this arrangement" (Yoga Vasishtha)

Reincarnation is Quite True (ii)

Kamlesh Kumari Devi, alias Gita Moorti, commenced preaching Gita at the age of two and a half years. She was born on Tuesday the 12th December 1939 The ideas of the transmigration of Soul and eternity of life, although recorded in our holy scriptures, are dormant and latent in our practical life

She used to sit in the lap of her father and pronounce the Slokas of Gita in her broken language

She used to glance at the Gita as well At the age of two and and half years her father Pundit Devi Dutt Sharma took her to the garden outside Lohgarh Gate, Amritsar, where Swami Krishnananda was holding discourses on Gita The Swami narrated the story of an eight year old girl at Allahabad who could recite the verse of Gita beautifully On hearing this Kamlesh Kumari felt excited and forced the Swami and the audience to hear her lecture on Gita She delivered her first lecture and deeply impressed the audience

Swami Krishnananda presented to her some Hindi books, Hindu Dharma, Parshisht etc, which she fluently read to the astonishment of the Swami After that she delivered lectures at Hardwar, Rishikesh, Ludhiana, Jandiala, Guru Har Sahai Mandi Mukherian, Dharma Kot, Gujranwala and other places

The other girl, Mahindra Kumari, alias Chand Rani, three and half years old, died in Tango Burma on 15-10-1939 and was reborn in Amritsar in May 1940 At the age of three and quarter years she forced her present mother to go to the house of her previous parents The girl went on insisting again and again, and importuned her mother every day to accompany her to visit her real house and real "Jahai". It is rightly said that persistence prevails and proved true in this case. At last the mother yielded, the baby led, and the mother followed her, to an unknown destination The baby girl took her mother from Mushkal Mohalla passing through the various streets and blind corners, brought her mother in Kucha Beriwala at the end of the street, before a house which she claimed as her own. When her previous life's brother's wife came from an adjoining house, on hearing the knocks and shouts at her door the baby girl recognised her Jahai, and ferociously embraced her by clinging to her legs, and subsequently recognised her 20 year old son Siva and other relatives and her belongings She recognised her gold Mutter Mala, and photo of her dead body saying that it was she who was sleeping. At the time of her death she had a great desire (Vasana) to see her brother S Sunder Singh, and his wife, who were not present at the time of her death and perhaps that deep-rooted Vasana at the time of leaving her body in Burma, led her to be reborn in Amritsar to meet her brother and his wife

Jain boy of Baroda (Statesman 5-9-37) In Baroda a Jain boy of six years surprised his mother by relating the incidents of his former life He said that he was previously at Poona of parents who belonged to Patna He was known as Kevalchand and later ran a drapery shop at Poona He had business relations with several merchants at Patna He had 6 sons, one of whom was named Ramanlal All these were verified when the boy and his mother visited Patna

The doctrine of reincarnation is supported by Guru Nanak Dev in Guru Granth Sahib as well as by the great philosophers of Greece such as Socrates and Plato who lived about 2400 years ago

"All our knowledge is a remembrance of what we have known only before we are born"—Platonic doctrine of reminiscence.

'We must have received our knowledge of all realities, before we were born Our souls existed formerly apart from our bodies and possessed intelligence before they came into man's shape"—Philosophy of Socrates

Bereft of the living self, this body dies while the living self dies not, because we find that when a man has fallen asleep leaving some work unfinished, when he wakes up, he remembers that he had left the work unfinished, and also just because creatures are born, they immediately evince a desire to suck the breast, terror, etc , it follows therefore, that they remember the sucking of the breast, and the pains experienced in the previous birth

Reincarnation in Lower Births

Ordinarily in most cases the Soul is not willing to take birth in the lower Yonis (wombs) for the salient reason that it has done good works in the physical body as a human being in the past incarnation No human being is out and out an incarnation of Lucifer Certain good qualities and actions prompted by such good qualities always outweigh the bad qualities and their actions and the human being steps into another birth either low or high out of the same species for the future evolution of the soul

The instances where the human Soul should take a lower birth either as a wolf or as a pig may be very few, just as in the physical world a murderer awaits his exist only through the doors of the gallows At the same time we cannot deny the truth of the scriptural texts, though they may be in some cases metaphorical with the sole object of deviating the human action from the bad to the good

The future birth of each soul is the result of its past actions and the theory of Karma and reincarnation play an important part in determining the same The law of cause and effect, action and reaction, holds good in the case of Karma also

Generally man evolves upwards. The tendency of the evolution is to take a man to a high level or status This is the natural biological law But there are exceptions If a man is endowed with devilish traits or Asuric tendencies and does highly brutal acts, if he behaves worse than an animal, if he acts like a dog or a donkey or a monkey, he surely does not deserve a human birth in the next life He will take birth in the womb of animals. He will be born as a dog or a monkey or a donkey. Such cases are, however, rare indeed

Even if man does heinous sins he can get the maximum punishment while dwelling in this physical body It is not necessary that he should take the birth of an animal Man suffers more for his sins while remaining in the body of a man than taking an animal birth. The sufferings of a leper, or a consumptive, a person suffering from syphilis, gonorrhoea are beyond description

The inexorable working of this law is brought out tellingly in the very unusual and extremely interesting case cited hereunder :—

Tarak, aged 18 or 19, compounder of Kaviraj Mahendranath Sen of Benda, got intense colic which drove him unconscious A Brahmin of Sarvavidya Lineage touched with pity, put vermillion on Tarak's forehead uttering Mantras and praying to Mother Kali to let him know why Tarak was suffering so badly

Tarak roared in his unconsciousness, "I am a part of Mother Kali Shall I not punish Tarak? In a past life he insulted his mother and his mother kicked her own husband, Tarak's father Both have been condemned to suffer for 7 births, Tarak from this terrible colic and his mother to become a widow only fourteen days after marriage They have had 4 births already and 3 more to suffer"

"Is there no means of deliverance, Mother?" asked the kind Brahmin

Tarak still unconscious replied "There can be no deliverance unless Tarak takes 'Padodak' of his mother and also 'Uchhishta' (the leaving of her food) and if his mother gives him medicine, he may be cured even in this life" On enquiring where Tarak's mother was, unconscious Tarak replied "Gopal Sen's widow is Tarak's mother"

Tarak came to his senses, heard everything from the Brahmin and obeyed the mandate. Tarak's mother gave him a portion of a 'Pan' (betel leaf) which Tarak wore in a 'Maduli' Tarak was cured straightaway

Next year the same disease returned but Tarak was cured when Tarak's mother sprinkled her 'Padodak' It was then found that Tarak's 'Maduli' had been defiled by taking water from a lady in her menses

Man learns lessons through bitter and painful experiences in this world However sinful, cruel and brutal a man may be, he corrects and educates himself through sufferings, pain sorrows, troubles and difficulties and diseases loss of property, poverty and death of dear and near relations God moulds and corrects the sinners in a mysterious manner Sufferings and pain act as useful educative forces They serve as eye-openers in the case of evil doers They check them from falling back and pull them upwards They begin to do good actions and seek the company of the saints

Some say that a man can never re-incarnate in an animal body, as his individuality cannot be conveniently accommodated by the insufficient and incapable body of an animal The higher principles of man can find no receptacle and expression in the rude, rough and imperfect habitation of the animal The body of a creature is always an encrustation, as it were, of its inner bodies which, too, are similarly of the same shape and cast Thus, the encrustation or body of a human soul should always be human It should correspond to the necessities, requirements and ambitions of a human soul It should be furnished with all the instruments of perception and conception, which a human soul stands in need of It should, in short, be cast upon the mould and matrix of the causal and astral bodies which generally form the plan and design of a human body Thus a human body cannot but incarnate in a human body The sayings of ancient writers that a cruel person will become a wolf, an avaricious person a cobra, a lustful person a bitch etc, are all metaphorical statements When they say that a cruel person will reincarnate as a wolf, they mean thereby that he will be re-born as a ferocious and voracious man like a wolf and similarly do other statements mean

Others hold the view that a man may try to fall back, nay, may do his best to live the life of a lower animal He may try to push out of his mind all higher and finer feelings and if he really succeeds in making a monkey of himself, if he succeeds in making his desires nothing but animal desires, and if he makes an animal of himself, then, of course, he will be born a monkey in the next incarnation But man cannot do that There are other forces which prevent and keep him back Those forces are what are called sorrow, trouble suffering etc They are the guaranteed agencies against any falling back These forces will not allow you to fall down, thus, progress is secured Life of evolution is progress and progress must be made and thus constant and continuous warfare are necessary

A human birth is the result of mixed Karmas, viz., good and bad When good Karmas outweigh the bad, man gets the birth of a Deva, Yaksha, Gandharva, and the like When evil Karmas outweigh the good he takes birth as an animal, devil etc He falls into a lower birth When good and bad Karmas are equal he gets a human birth By good Karmas man attains heaven, by bad Karmas hell and by mixed Karmas he attains the world of men

It is the nature of a man or a beast to get attached to the particular body in which it resides The body of an ant is as dear to it as the body of an elephant is to an elephant or a human body is to a man This wonderful attachment to the body arising out of ignorance keeps this wheel of birth and death eternally going Of all births a particular creature likes the particular body which it has taken in the particular incarnation A man likes a human birth, an elephant is pleased with its birth as an elephant and so on At the same time everyone craves for evolution and attainment of unalloyed bliss This is common for all created beings

Birth as a man is superior because he has the power to discriminate and decide for himself He knows himself and others and he is endowed with finer emotions of love, faith, shame, decency, non-injury, etc An animal is devoid of intelligence, memory and knowledge Therefore birth as an animal is not desirable

The life of a man who is not endowed with discrimination, knowledge of the Self, non-identification with the physical body, faith and love for fellow-beings, is equal to that of a beast The ignorant man sinks in the ocean of Samsara, and takes births in various wombs until the eye of discrimination is opened, until he comes in contact with a guide who is ready to take him to a higher path The ignorant worldly man takes birth as a dog, a cobra, a wolf or a tiger There is no definite law as regards them The Shastras are quite correct in their statements It is a serious mistake to take such utterances of the scriptures as merely figurative or metaphorical

A spiritual Sadhak who has started his life in the Divine has no fear of birth in a lower womb A

Yogi who practises Yoga even though he happens to fall from his entitled position is not ruined He takes both birth in better circumstances once again and pursues his spiritual path In Bhagavad Gita you will find 'O Partha, neither in this world, nor in the next world is there destruction for him (who is fallen from the path of Brahman), none verily, who does good, O my son, ever comes to grief Having attained to the worlds of the righteous and having dwelt there for everlasting years, he who fell from Yoga is reborn in a house of the pure and wealthy Or he is born in a family of even the wise Yogis" (Chapter VI—40, 41, 42)

King Bharata, son of Rishabha, renounced his kingdom and took to the path of an ascetic One day he observed a small motherless deer in the forest He took pity on the poor creature and he so passionately loved the little one that his thoughts were mainly centred on the deer and thoughts of God gradually waned away At the time of his death the thought of the small deer harassed him much and he took the birth of a deer

King Bharata was well versed in all the scriptures, in Vedas and the Puranas He did very rigorous Tapas and meditated on the lotus feet of the glorious Vasudeva But the inordinate attachment to the animal gave him the birth of a deer Bharata opened his eyes and recognised his folly The deer remembered every detail of the past life as King Bharata It ever meditated on the Lord, ate but little and never mixed with other deers of its type It was actually counting the number of days of its life to get freedom from the low birth The deer after leaving its body again took the birth of a Brahmin known by the name Jada Bharata Now Jada Bharata grew wise enough as not to commit the same mistake once again and from his very boyhood kept himself aloof He had a mind free from attraction and repulsion Thus he escaped the clutches of Maya and at the dissolution of his mortal sheath attained oneness with the Paramatman

Gajendra though he had to take the birth of an elephant, never forgot his real nature and ever prayed to Lord Hari and attained emancipation from the life of an elephant itself Our Shastras quote instances where animals and even birds had attained emancipation Vratrasura, the great Rakshasa, was highly devoted to Vasudeva He was King Chitraketu in his past birth who was cursed by Uma to become a Rakshasa

From the foregoing examples it is quite clear that for a true and sincere Sadhak there is no fear of downfall Devotees of the Lord become absolutely fearless and they are devoid of all desires They welcome any birth in which the Lord can be remembered

What is wanted is real devotion to the Lord That being achieved, a man becomes happy in any sort of life and under any circumstances He gets a peculiar joy which helps him to bear even the most excruciating pain of Samsara

The Rishis of yore had power to curse wicked persons and bless the virtuous The sons of Kubera became trees by the curse of Narada. Gautama cursed his wife Ahalya to become a stone [illegible]

out of compassion for those who go astray, leaving the feet of Lord Hari It is not with any selfish motive or by becoming a victim to anger that they curse the wicked Therefore, contact with a saintly personality is highly beneficial in changing one's destiny

Rishis are Trikalajnanis (knowers of the past, present and future) Therefore, they know the mysterious ways of Karma They attained knowledge of the Self and by virtue of this knowledge everything else became known to them

It does not matter much what kind of body we wear It matters much what our thoughts are A man of high position may have the thoughts of a beast When he becomes a prey to lust and anger he is worse than an animal A cow is thousand times better than such a man who is devoid of discrimination, who indulges in vulgar enjoyments, who loses his temper for trifles

Do not worry yourself as to what birth you will take in the future Utilise the present life profitably and free yourself from death and birth Develop devotion to the Lord Renounce base desires. Be ever intent on doing good to others. Be kind and do good.

Lord Hari is the protector of the three worlds The responsibility of taking every one of his creation to His immortal abode rests with Him Let Him take you through any path He likes Let Him give you Mukti when you are in the body of a man, a beast or a devil Let your mind be ever centred on Him and cling to His lotus feet like the bee that sticks to a full blown lotus Drink the sweet honey flowing from

His lotus feet and surrender yourself to him like a child

May you all become free from this ever revolving wheel of Karma resulting in numerous births in various wombs and attain the bliss of the Immortal in this very life

Development of the Child

Having fallen in the lunar orb and mixed with vapour he comes down upon earth, there he remains in rice and the rest, for a long time

Then he becomes the four-fold kind of food and is eaten by man and becoming the vital seed, is thrown by man into the womb of the woman when the season comes *

There in the mother's womb mixed with blood and enveloped in the outer skin of the embryo, he becomes what is known as 'kalal' in one day

On the expiration of five nights he becomes a budbud (bubble) At the end of seven nights he attains the condition of a lump of flesh *(mamsapeshi)*.

---

*The allusion here is to the Panchagni Vidya of the Upanishads The passage of the Jiva mentioned here is from this world to the moon, thence to Parjanya (god presiding over rain), thence again to this world through rain, thence to man in whom the product of rain in the shape of grain and other eatables enters and thence into woman in whom the vital seed is thrown by man These are the five fires through which gods pour libations before one becomes known as man.

At the end of a fortnight that lump of flesh becomes filled with blood and at the expiration of 25 nights it sprouts forth

At the end of one month are produced in it the neck, the head, the shoulder, the spine and the belly. Each of these five organs is produced one after the other

In two months are produced in due order and not otherwise, the hands, the feet, the sides, the hips, the thighs and knees

In three months are produced gradually the joints of the body All the fingers are produced gradually in four months

The nose, the ears and the eyes are produced in the fifth month The rows of the teeth, the nails, the secret organs are also produced in five months

After the sixth month are produced the holes in the ears In the same month are also produced the anus, the organs of generation, male and female, and the navel amongst human beings.

In the seventh month are produced hair on the body as well as the hair on the head

In the eighth month all the organs of the body become divided.

In this manner the foetus increases in the womb of the woman In the fifth month the embodied being becomes possessed of intelligence on all sides

Through a small hole in the navel cord the creature derives its sustenance in the womb from the essence of what the mother eats and does not die because of its Karma.

Remembering all his former births and his former actions burning in the fire of the digestive organs, he utters the following —

'Becoming born in thousands of diverse births, I have enjoyed my connection with millions of sons, wives and relations

Attached to rearing up the family I earned wealth through fair and foul means Unfortunate am I that I did not think of Vishnu even in a dream

Now I am reaping the fruit thereof in the shape of dire misery in this womb Burning with desire and taking this unreal body for the reality I did what I ought not to have done and failed to do what was for my own good

Having in this way suffered misery of diverse kinds through my own Karma when shall I get out of this womb which is like unto hell Henceforth I will worship no one else but Vishnu"

Thinking of this and the like manner the Jiva, pained by the pressure of the mother's organs, comes out with great trouble like a sinner from hell

Like a worm from a festering sore he comes out

Then he suffers the troubles of the conditions of childhood, youth, old age, and the rest

CHAPTER SIX

LOKAS OR PLANES

Preta Loka

A passionate man, whose mind is filled with lower appetites and strong sense-cravings, who has spent his life in much sensual indulgence in this earth-plane, enters the Preta Loka after his death. He is unconscious for a short time after death He is in a sleepy state He awakens and finds himself in this Loka or world

As soon as he wakes up, the sensual cravings desires and appetites torment him immensely He wants to eat, drink and enjoy with women But he cannot gratify his desires now with his present body. He is kept in this world [illegible] as in the prison Therefore, he is extremely miserable and unhappy, as he cannot gratify his passion in this plane. The senses are powerful, but he cannot get here the means of gratification His misery is beyond description as he is not able to satisfy his passions, cravings and appetites He is just like a starving man.

The passions have their roots and centres in the senses and the mind They are not in the physical body. This physical body is only the instrument of gratification in the hands of the senses and the mind.

You can help the sufferer in the Preta Loka by performing Sraddha Performance of Sraddha helps to free him and make him pass on to Swarga or the heaven The Mantras recited set up powerful vibrations These vibrations come against the body which imprisons the individual soul and break it

Do you realise now the importance of Sraddha? Those who have left doing Sraddha on account of ignorance, perversion of intellect caused by wrong Samskaras and bad association and hearing of wrong teaching, should perform Sraddha from this moment at least. Rishis and Shastras take care of you like kind mothers

If you do not wish to enter the Preta Loka and undergo the sufferings, learn to be wise Learn to control the senses Lead a well-regulated and disciplined life Do not allow the senses to run riot. Give up gluttony Do not follow the philosophy of flesh Passions and appetites will only torment you when you pass through death. If you practise self-restraint, you will enter the regions of bliss.

Experience of Pretas

Vasishtha says in his Yoga Vasishtha

"The Pretas are of six kinds, namely, the slightly sinful, the ordinarily sinful, the greatly sinful, the slightly virtuous, the ordinarily virtuous, and the greatly virtuous Some of the most sinful Pretas continue to be experiencing the insensibility of death like a stone for a period of a year. Regaining awareness they experience that they are doomed to suffer from the endless torments of hell which their Vasa has have brought them, for a long time They then undergo the experience of hundreds of incarnations until they finally get rid of the experience of world-illusion, by finding peace within There are others in this class who, after their torpor of death is over, begin to experience the unutterable pain of insensibility in the form of immovable trees, etc. Then they undergo the torments of hell, after which they are again born on earth in accordance with their earthly desires Those of ordinary sin experience the inertness of stone for some time after death Being awakened to consciousness, they, then or after some time, undergo the experience of the lives of birds, reptiles or beasts, before they turn to their usual lives in the world The slightly sinful souls, often immediately after the insensibility of death, come to assume some human form to continue their earthly existence in accordance with their previous desires They come to the worldly consciousness soon after their death and their previous desires and imagination [illegible] new worlds in their experience in a dream-like manner The greatly virtuous souls, soon after the insensibility of death is over, get an experience in the worlds of gods Having enjoyed the fruits of their virtues in godly personality and in heavenly worlds, they are again born in this world in noble and rich families The souls of ordinary virtuous, experience, after the insensibility of death is over, that they are being carried away by winds and later on are turned into the lives of plants and herbs. Having undergone this experience for some time they feel that they are entering human bodies as food, and there they are turned into spermatozoa and thence enter the wombs of (expectant) mothers"

Pitri Loka

This is also known by the name Chandraloka wherein the forefathers or Pitris live This is also a heaven Those who perform sacrifies and charitable deeds with selfish motives (Ishtapurtam) such as digging wells, building rest-houses and laying out parks or gardens for the public enter this Loka The ruler of this world is Lord Yama, son of Surya The Jivas come back to this world after the fruits of their actions have been exhausted Lord Krishna says in Gita "Smoke night time, the dark fortnight also (the six months of the southern path of the sun) attaining by these to the lunar light, the Yogi returns.—Chap VIII-25 When they die, they first go through smoke, then to night, then to the dark fifteen days, then to the six months when the sun goes to the South and from that they go to the world of their fathers This path is called by the name Pitriyana or the path of Pitris

The Pitris are highly pleased when their descendants offer oblations and when they perform Sraddha on the anniversary day, they bless them

In Chandraloka the Jivas acquire fine brilliant bodies, the bodies of gods They become gods and enjoy the happiness of heaven for a long period They live with their forefathers They come down through the spheres of air and clouds They reach this world through rain drops They attach themselves to some cereal or grain, which is eaten by some man, who is fit to give them material to make a new body Those whose deeds have been very good take birth in good families

The heaven of the Fathers or Pitri-loka or Chandraloka is not the highest abode of eternal Truth It is phenomenal universe The dwellers of that Loka or plane are bound by the Law of Karma by the cause and effect, by the law of action and reaction Their stay on that plane is temporary although it may last for thousands of years

The Pitris have no knowledge of Brahman or the Imperishable Soul They are bound by desires They cannot teach Brahma-Vidya to others as they themselves are imperfect

Lord Krishna says in the Bhagavad Gita —

"The knowers of the three, the Soma drinkers, the purified from sin, worshipping Me with sacrifice, pray to Me the way to heaven, they, ascending to the holy world of the Ruler of the Shining Ones, eat in heaven the divine feasts of the Shining Ones"

"They, having enjoyed the spacious heaven-world, their holiness withered, come back to this world of death Following the virtues enjoined by the three, desiring desires, they obtain the transitory"

"They who worship the Shining Ones go to the Shining Ones to the ancestors go the ancestor-worshippers, to the Elements go those who sacrifice to Elements, but My worshippers come unto Me"

"Even the dwellers of the highest heavens are subject to the laws of rebirth and reincarnation He alone is free from birth and rebirth and transcends all phenomena who, after knowing the Absolute Truth, after realising the Supreme Soul. becomes one with Brahman or the Absolute"

Heaven or Svarga

The conception of heaven of the Hindus is different from that of the Christians or of the Mohammedans Heaven of the Hindus is a place where the departed souls go to reap the fruits of their virtuous deeds. They remain there for some time till the fruits of their virtuous actions are exhausted Then they come back to the world They eat in heaven the divine feasts of the Shining Ones or the Devas They move in celestial cars Indra is the Lord of the heaven or Svarga Various kinds of Devas dwell here Celestial damsels like Urvasi, Rambha dance here The Gandharvas sing There is no disease here There is no trouble of hunger and thirst The inhabitants are endowed with a Tejasic or brilliant subtle body They are adorned with shining garments Heaven is a thought-world Whatever one wishes, he gets it at once. So it is a happier world than the earth-plane

The Christians, Mohammedans and Zoroastrians believe in heaven of all kinds of sense-enjoyments The departed souls pass through the bridge Al Sirat The faithful ones who have done virtuous deeds reach the Paradise which is situated in heaven The Mohammedan conception of Paradise is that of a beautiful garden, furnished with springs, fountains and rivers flowing with water, milk, honey and balsam. There are trees having their trunks of gold and yielding the most delicious fruits There are seventy effulgent, beautiful girls called Hur-ul-ayun with big black eyes The Jews and the Zoroastrians also have a similar conception of heaven

The Paradise of the Zoroastrians are known by the names Bihisht and Minu The persons who have done good deeds in the earth-plane enjoy the company of Huran-i-bihisht or black-eyed damsels of paradise who are under the care of the angel Zamiyad The name for heaven is Garo-de-mana (Garot-man in the Persian) or house of hymns The angels sing hymns here, just as Gandharvas sing in the heaven of the Hindus

The Jews and the Parsis believe in seven Heavens The heaven of Eden is composed of precious stones There is a resemblance between the garden of Eden and the paradise of Zoroastrians The two trees in Eden, the tree of knowledge and the tree of life, correspond to the painless tree and the Gao Karena bearing the white Roama

The Parsis, the Christians and Mohammedans believe that heaven is eternal and permanent All enjoyments come to them incessantly without any pain or difficulty.

Heaven also is a place of sensual enjoyment The enjoyments in heaven are more intense, subtle and refined They cannot give everlasting peace and real eternal bliss They will wear out the senses A wise man with discrimination and dispassion will never crave for the enjoyments of heaven He will never dream to have an abode in heaven. There is jealousy; there is Raga-Dvesha (likes and dislikes) in heaven.

Asuras fight with gods Real thirsty aspirants should ruthlessly ignore heaven They should yearn for the final emancipation or Moksha

Every man builds up his own heaven according to his own desires and imaginations Every man has his own idea of pleasures Pleasures are always changing A drunkard dreams of a heaven where there are rivers of wine This would be a very bad heaven for a sober, pious man A young man dreams of a heaven where he will have celestial damsels, celestial cars fine music and dance When that man becomes old he does not want a woman It is your necessities and desires that make your heaven

You have no idea of real eternal bliss of the Soul Your mind whirls in sensual pleasures That is the reason why you are carried away by thoughts of heaven or paradise Have a clear understanding of the nature of the Soul You will have no craving for the enjoyments of heaven Atman or the Soul is an ocean of bliss The ocean of bliss or the fountain of joy is within you Withdraw the senses Look within Fix the mind on the Soul All sensual desires will melt You will be immersed in the ocean of bliss

The period for which you live in heaven depends upon the degree of your meritorious deeds You can become an Indra or Lord of the heaven if you like Indrahood is a position The Indra who had lived before is not the Indra of the present day. Countless Indras have come and gone

When man becomes disgusted with the world around him through miseries sorrows, disappointments, failures, loss of property, diseases and death or dearest relatives, he thinks that he would go to some place where there would be all happiness for ever without any misery or pain where he would live with his forefathers with a perfect body So he creates heaven or Svargas How can there be eternal happiness in a finite plane conditioned in time and space? Eternal bliss and immortality can be found in your own Atman or Self only

A life in heaven is very much the same sort of life you lead here, only a little happier You have comfortable living there, but it is not eternal life of everlasting bliss Further, you will have to come down to earth-plane when the fruits of good actions are exhausted Heaven is not a permanent abode. Everything which has name and form must perish. Atman or Soul only is immortal and eternal. That is the reason why sages and thirsty aspirants after Truth do not long for the enjoyments of heaven

Vedanta does not attach any special value to heaven It teaches that these heavens are phenomenal and transitory Even if one dwells in heaven for millions of years, these millions of years are nothing before eternity

Lord Jesus says, "The Kingdom of Heaven is within you" Vedanta also tells the same thing. Real everlasting happiness can be attained by realising one's own Atman or the Immortal Soul. Eternal bliss is within Perennial joy is in your own innermost Self. The little pleasure that you get from objects is only reflection of the bliss of the soul It is a particle of that real eternal bliss of soul

Man sees God face to face He lives in God There is no intervening veil or limitation between him and the Lord He lives in absolute and complete oneness with Him He is ever blissful This is Heaven

From the transcendental viewpoint, there is neither heaven nor hell They are mental creations only If your mind is filled with Sattva, you are in heaven If Tamas and Rajas preponderate in your mind, you are in hell.

When a man who has done meritorious actions dies, he becomes a Deva or God and dwells in heaven. He enjoys various kinds of pleasures in heaven During his period of stay in heaven he does not do any fresh Karma or action Dwelling in heaven is simply a reward for his past good actions. In the Deva form he does not perform any Karma at all

Abandon the idea of heaven The idea of obtaining eternal happiness in heaven is a vain dream It is puerile idea Seek the eternal bliss in your own Atman through meditation You are the Immortal Soul, free, eternal, you are ever pure, ever blessed Assert your birth-right Proclaim your freedom and be what you really are, ever free, ever blessed. Everything in time, space and causation is bound. The Soul is beyond all time, all space, all causation 'Tat Twam Asi, Thou art That my child Realise this and be ever happy.

Lord Buddha says. "Many thousand myriads of systems of worlds beyond this is a region of bliss called Sukhavati This region is encircled within seven rows of railings, seven rows of vast curtains seven rows of waving trees This holy abode of the Arhats is governed by the Tathagatas and is occupied by the Bodhisattvas It has seven precious lakes, in the midst of which flow crystalline waters having seven and yet one distinctive properties and qualities This, O Sariputra, is the Devachan Its divine Udumbara flower casts a root in the shadow of every earth, and blossoms for all those who reach it Those born in this blessed region—who have crossed the golden bridge and reached the seven golden mountains —they are truly felicitous, there is no more grief or sorrow in that cycle for them"

Only persons who have earned great merits on earth can go to heaven The heaven is well provided with excellent paths It is always frequented by celestial cars Atheists and untruthful persons, those who have not performed asceticism and those who have not performed great sacrifices, cannot go there

Only virtuous souls and those of subdued minds, those who have controlled their senses, those who are free from malice, those intent on the practice of charity, and heroes and men bearing marks of battle and who have performed the most meritorious acts, attain to the celestial regions The celestial regions can be attained only by virtuous acts The celestial regions are inhabited by pious men They bestow every object of desire The Siddhas, the Viswas, the Gandharvas, the Apsaras, the Yamas and the Dhamas, dwell there There is that foremost of mountains, the golden Meru, extending to thirty thousand Yojanas There are many celestial gardens The Nandana garden is the most beautiful one Here sport the persons of meritorious acts Neither hunger nor thirst, nor heat, nor cold, neither grief nor fatigue, neither labour nor repentance, nor fear, nor anything that is disgusting and inauspicious, is found There is no old age either

Delightful fragrance is found everywhere The breeze is gentle and pleasant The inhabitants have resplendent bodies Delightful sounds captivate both the ear and the mind These worlds are obtained by meritorious acts, and not by birth or the merits of fathers and mothers

There is neither sweat nor stench, nor excretion, nor urine The dust does not soil one's clothes There is no uncleanliness of any kind Garlands do not fade Excellent garments full of celestial fragrance, never fade There are countless celestial cars that move in the air The dwellers are free from envy, grief, ignorance, and malice They live very happily

Such is the bliss of heaven But the disadvantages of heaven are great indeed. In the celestial region a person, while enjoying the fruits of acts he had already performed, cannot perform any other new act He must enjoy the fruits of the former life till they are completely exhausted Further he is liable to fall after he has completely exhausted his merit These are the disadvantages of heaven The consciousness of those about to fall is stupefied. It is also agitated by emotions As the garlands of those about to fall fade away, fear possesses their hearts

But there is one world where there are no such disadvantages It is the supreme seat of Vishnu, above the abode of Brahma, which is pure, eternal, and effulgent. It is known by the name of Para Brahman

Persons who are addicted to sensual objects or those who are subject to arrogance, covetousness, ignorance, anger and envy cannot go to that place Those men who are free from conflicting emotions and those who have restrained their senses and those who are given to meditation and Yoga can go there

Men who enjoy heaven suffer great misery and extreme regret in this world Therefore do not desire to go to heaven Try to reach that supreme abode of eternal bliss from where there will be no fall. Seek that unfailing region, going to which people have not to lament, or to be pained, or to be agitated

Practise Jnana Yoga Engage yourself in constant meditation on Para Brahman or the Supreme Self Attain knowledge of the Imperishable and obtain the supreme state of emancipation, which is eternal Then censure and praise will become equal to you A brick, a stone, and a piece of gold—all will become the same to you

Hell or Naraka

It is common now-a-days to hear it said that the Puranas are very unreliable scriptures and that they indulge in unlimited exaggeration about very many things. These critics say that the Puranas contain gross overstatements and preposterously puerile attempts to cajole or to cow down the reader with citations like the grandiose descriptions of heavenly regions and their joys as also of the aweful pictures of hell-fires and its torments To criticise a subject requires very little wit or wisdom For simple and direct condemnation without caring to consider the pros and cons of a matter is the inborn nature of the human mind But even to these biased ones a little thoughtful consideration will forthwith reveal that the sagely writers of the Puranas had a special purpose in writing certain thing in the manner they did They deliberately emphasised and layed particular stress upon some subjects with a definite end in view, Underneath these graphic and detailed descriptions of the Karmas and their consequences there is a shrewd psychology and insight being put to make a practical purpose

Until and unless Self-realisation is attained, Knowledge Absolute is gained, there is ever the ebb and flow, the constant see-saw between the animal and the man in every human being The beast or the brute is never completely absent or overcome except through a final Divinisation of the individual As long as there is the human, side by side there will be the animal also, now the one having the upper hand now the other It is only when the Jiva gets above and beyond both these and gets transformed and established in the third and hitherto dormant aspect of his nature, namely the Divine aspect, that he becomes "Mriga-Nara-Atita" Then onwards there is no more of this tug-of-war between the animal and man natures to gain precedence and dominate over the field of Jiva-consciousness For now the Divine Kshetrajna Himself reigns supreme over the Kshetra

Now until this state is attained we find therefore that man is in turn animal and human according to the Vritti that possesses him He shows himself alternately to be noble and petty. He swings between the sublime and the bathos His two different aspects react to the external stimuli in their own distinctive manners And equally likewise only particular modes of external approach succeed in evoking the desired response from these dual aspects in man's consciousness Thus it is that we find in persons who have evolved themselves to some fair extent and acquired a good measure of Sattva, of refinement, culture and character, the purely gross and degenerate impulses and temptations fail to have effect They succeed only in exceptional situations when the person unfortunately happens to be in some rare moment of weakness due to a revival of Samskaras Whereas in gross natures such temptations readily and immediately work havoc, and vice versa, noble impulses immediately influence a fine nature but fail to evoke any response in a gross person of low animal mentality This has given rise to the proverb in the Marathi language "To the cobbler's deity worship is by shoes," or again the current Tamil saying "Without the cane the monkey will not dance" The same is the case with noble sentiments too, as is simply exemplified by the overcareful psychology applied by the famous Dr Arnold of Rugby in appealing to the worthier instincts in his boys No less striking is the historic example of Mark Antony skilfully exercising his persuative and provocatory eloquence upon his Roman audience, first to evoke compassion by playing subtly upon their human side, and then rousing a frenzy of revengeful violence by inflaming their strong animal passion of anger.

It is this deep human insight and admirable penetrating psychology that is at the basis of the Hell and Retribution ideas in the Puranic Hindu Religion. They knew that sweet whistling will not make the buffalo move, whereas whipping will. We know how on the eve of building the great bridge to Lanka, when requests failed to make the Ocean-King behave suitably, Rama took out an arrow in anger The very next instant had the Sagara-Raja pleading with folded hands before Rama Likewise to goad man on to noble deeds, high aspiration and righteous conduct, the Puranic sages held out before him bright prospects and extolled the untold benefits and blessings of a good life Here they tried to appeal to man's human side But when he indulged in extreme sin and bestial acts of gross sensuality, they knew it was not the occasion for mincing matters. The beast could only be chastened through a true and vivid description of the inevitable results of his actions Here we must note that they did not exaggerate or utter any falsehood, but gave a special importance to emphasise the matter by dilating upon it in graphic detail and spared no pains in doing this They therefore confronted the Jiva with a terrific array of dire consequences that would inevitably accrue to the evil actions of the sinner. They gave graphic descriptions of the various punishments awaiting the wanton transgressor of moral and spiritual laws They vividly related past instances of transgressors and the retribution that overtook them to testify to this truth The Puranas abound in fearful examples of life-long sufferings in lower wombs suffered by people like Nahusha, Java and Vijaya, the well-known Gajendra and many others

They do not stop with that As though it were not enough to give instances of the "Phalas" of positive sinful actions and crimes, they cite certain cases when even the indulgence in a comparatively harmless, good emotion like affection, brings about grave suffering upon man The warning implied in the story of the past lives of Sage Jadabharata is an instance in point Also the accidental participation in a seeming falsehood was enough to send a soul to take a sight, though but for a moment, of the awful hell-fire The incident of the great Yudhishthira's Naraka-Darshan is referred to here

Fortunately or unfortunately, out of the numerous Puranas very few are studied by the vast majority now-a-days Those few devoted people that read the Puranas or listen to their recital rarely go beyond the four or five classical Saivite and Vaishnavite Puranas that are popularly current throughout the country We may say that Purana perusal is generally confined to the Skanda, Markandeya, Vishnu or the Srimad Bhagavata It is not the scholar or the orthodox Brahmin section that is meant here but the common man-in-the-street who goes to form a distinct and important part of the population Thus this whip-crack of the Karma and Karma-phala citation does not sound now-a-days to chasten the sensual beast in man And as a result of this it is running amuck as never heretofore But laws, be they mundane or divine are inexorable The ignorance of the Penal Code does not lay a premium on indulgence in crime nor does the offender go scot-free He burgles and he gets jailed He murders and is hanged Likewise also he sins and he suffers If this truth of the inescapable order of cosmic Law is placed before him in unvarnished and distinct outline it may serve just a little bit to persuade him to give up vice and follow virtue, to renounce Adharma and embrace Dharma It has purposes confined mainly to the physical and mental forms that this heavenly retribution takes, and also to the forms it takes upon this earth-plane For modern man is held by the motto "seeing is believing" and he hardly requires to give a second glance to show the terrible truth of the price man pays in hospitals and clinics for the crimes against Dharma

The disease we suffer from, the births we get here on earth are all products of actions done by us in previous times Every action has its reaction and no action goes unrewarded in a suitable manner Evil actions do not go without their bitter effects upon the doer

Hells are not an imaginary fiction as ordinarily conceived of by the modern rationalistic mind The empiricist believes only in experience of sense-contact and feels himself unable to rise above the dictates of the intellect But it does not mean that man has reason to overlook facts beyond his comprehension We have no right to assert that this globe of earth is the most concrete reality and that others are mere apparitions The stars do not become mere spots with a twinkling light in the sky merely for the reason that we perceive them to be so If I have not seen America I have no right to deny the existence of such a country There are evidences, both intuitional and rational, for us to accept the existence of worlds beyond which are entirely different both in nature and size The Yogavasishtha says that our earth is only an atom among many other larger worlds existing beyond our perception and is of one particular variety among many others which differ from it in every way We have no authority to discard the account given by Vasishtha that there exist worlds which are made of different materials like copper iron gold, etc, filled with water, milk and the like, and inhabited by serpents, animals, devils, and so on It is not necessary that human beings alone should inhabit all worlds and that the same earthly conditions should prevail in all planes of existence The universe is a gradual revelation of the Infinite Absolute in various degrees of Consciousness, which is inclusive of every sort of life and experience The Infinite is a great Wonder and we cannot say what things are thriving in its womb ' We and our world are but one among the many in it ' There are many families in Infinity and earth, hell heaven, men animals, gods, devils are all Its children with varying temperaments The Absolute ranges from lowest matter to Pure Bliss or Ananda, and between these exist the countless universes with their contents They differ both in their individual nature and in the nature of their contents It is said that beings take birth in one or the other of these worlds in accordance with their actions which bear fruits of a kind that can be reaped only in that particular world Only fire can give heat and only food can appease hunger Even so only a particular condition and environment can enable as to reap the fruits of a specific action Though punishments need not necessarily be due to the wrath of any personal Divine Being, it can be asserted that it is necessary, by the very law of nature, that the soul should manifest itself with a body suited for its experience determined by its past actions As such, it is not unreasonable that variety in the nature of worlds should be real We have to remember that the real is unseen

Hells, therefore, are as much real worlds as the regions of Indra or this mortal earth of ours They are regions with difference only in the subtlety of the plane of their manifestation They differ in the degree of the state of Consciousness revealed through them The sufferings inflicted on the sinners may be taken to mean either an actual birth in such regions or a life on earth with such entanglements, where one will undergo such pains either directly or through the agency of others

In the Vedas and Vedanta there is no mention of hell The Puranas only speak of hell or place of torture From the absolute viewpoint, there is neither heaven nor hell It is all mental creation From the relative viewpoint, hell is as much real as this world For a man of discrimination, this world also is a hell. Hell and heaven, though not absolutely real are not unreal as long as individuality persists, and are as much as any plane of existence

Christians and Mohammedans speak of eternal hell. There cannot be eternal damnation or eternal punishment The life of a wicked man here is nothing when compared with eternal life If there be an eternal damnation into the fire, it means that there is an infinite effect produced by a finite cause. This cannot be

The different torments of hell, the seven compartments into which it is said to be divided, and the partition called Al Airat separating heaven from hell according to Mohammedanism, all seem to be copied from the Jews

Hindu Puranas have been very clear on the question of heaven and hell Writers of law books or Smritis, like Yajnavalkya and Vishnu, have given serious description of the various hells and the various pleasures of heaven Yogi Yajnavalkya mentions 21 hells in his law book viz, Raurava, Kumbhipaka, Maharaurava, Tamisra, Andha Tamisara, etc The author of Vishnu Smriti also has written the same thing A hell is a region of sharp, severe, intense pain The evil-doers suffer for a period. Bad action is worked out in that state and then the evil-doers come back to earth-plane They get another chance

The Ruler of Hell is Lord Yama He is assisted by Chitragupta Hell is a particular locality which is walled off from the surrounding regions of space by the messengers of Yama Sinners get a thick body called 'Yatana-deha' when they are punished The punishment in hell is not remembered by the soul when it is reborn The punishment in hell is reformatory and educative The permanent educative effect remains in conscience. The innate fear which some souls feel at the sight of temptation of sin is due to the finer development of conscience in the furnace of hell-fire This is the permanent gain acquired by the soul The soul is reborn with keener conscience after being purified by Hell-fire He can make better use of his faculties in the next birth

The Jewish belief in a future life in Heaven and Hell coincides in all its detail with what we find in the Zend Avesta and is borrowed from it There is a similarity in the Parsi and Jewish accounts of hell and its sevenfold divisions The doctrine of eternal reward and punishment of the Jews is also borrowed from the Zend Avesta Gatha Ushtavaiti says "The soul of the righteous attains to immortality, but that of the wicked man has everlasting punishment Such is the rule of Ahura Mazda, whose the creatures are"

If the mind is filled with Rajas and Tamas, this state is hell only Prison is physical hell only To live in this cage of flesh without practising Japa and meditation is hell only

Repentance for sin with a contrite heart is the highest Prayaschitta The evil effects of sins are exhausted by repentance Fasting, charity, penance, Japa meditation, Kirtan destroy all sins Thus a man may save himself from the pains of hell

Lord Krishna says in Gita "Triple is the gate of this hell destruction of the Self—lust, anger and greed, therefore let man renounce these three" (XVI-21) You do various wicked deeds when you are under the influence of anger, lust and greed If you control these three evil Vrittis, you enjoy everlasting peace Cultivate the opposite virtues of forgiveness, purity and generosity, these evil traits will die by themselves

Karma and Hells

There are varieties of hells that a Jiva has to experience in accordance with the Karmas which he does through sin and passion Twenty-nine kinds of regions of suffering are described in the Bhagavata, when Jivas are said to be born due to their Karmas

There is a place of suffering called Tamisra Those people who lay hands on another's wealth, children and wives, are born in this region The Jiva experiences there extreme pain being bound with mortal cords and violently hurled into the dark regions He has no food or drink He is beaten with clubs, and by holding out threats and being brought to a state of weary affliction the Jiva drops down in a swoon

There is another region called the Andhatamisra (blinding darkness) Here Jivas are born who deceive husbands and appropriate to themselves their wives and other property Such Jivas are cast down into this hell to suffer torments where they lose all understanding and sense through excessive pain. The Jiva suffers like a tree whose roots are cut

Those who grossly identify themselves with this physical body and regard the wealth of the world as their own, fall into a hell called Raurava Those people who torment people here on earth become subject to the torment of poisonous worms called Rurus in this dangerous region

Maharaurava is one of the same type Those men who indulge in passions are eaten here by carnivorous (flesh-eating) animals

In the hell called Kumbhipaka, dreadful fiends begin to boil in oil that cruel and merciless person who cooks and eats living animals, birds and the like

He is thrown into a hell called Kalasutra who insults spiritual men, Brahmins, and Pitris He is placed on the surface of burning copper, forty-thousand miles in extent and constantly heated by fire below and the sun above, and being tormented by hunger and thirst, undergoes untold misery

There is a hell called Asipatravan This is a forest full of leaves made out of sharp daggers The Jiva is made to run through the forest and is hunted like a beast He who goes against the Vedic Dharma, who embraces infidelistic religions is thrown here ! Oh pitiable sight ! indeed he runs this way and that way and has every part of his body torn up in those dreadful woods of sword The Jiva cries out 'Ah ! I am undone" and falls down in agony.

Kings who inflict punishment on innocent men, or who inflict corporeal punishment to a Brahmin, fall into the hell called Sukara-Mukta There every part of the body of the sinner is crushed like sugar-canes ! He shrieks in distress but none helps him

Those men who having a good position in society inflict pain upon other poor people fall into a hell called Andhakupa The Jiva is tormented on all sides in darkness by varieties of terrible beasts, serpents, etc , and learns such lessons that will not allow him to do such sinful actions again

Brahmins who do not perform their daily Yajnas, who do not share with others what they possess are fie to be called crows and fall into a hell where their food are worms They are cast down into a vast ocean of worms where they begin to tease the Jiva from all sides

Who robs a Brahmin or a poor man and thus causes him to suffer without reason, falls into a hell where he is severely pinched by burning iron tongs and hit by red-hot iron balls

Those men or women who abuse innocent poor servants and coolies who are rather to be pitied and helped for their miserable condition, fall into a hell where they are severely thrashed and forced to embrace a burning image of iron like unto a man or woman Those who abuse their marriage-beds are given a similar punishment

Whoever here approaches under the force of passion all kinds of beings, is placed in the Salmali Hell with adamantine thorns and is dragged through the region of hell

Kings who transgress the limits of righteousness, and administrative employees who discard the law of justice fall into the river Vaitarani after their death. The Jivas are bitten by aquatic monsters but are not separated from their body and are on the other hand supported by their vital breaths to be ever alive to the consequences of their Karma This river is flooded with refuse, urine, pus, blood, hair, nails, bones, marrow, flesh and fat

Those men born of a higher caste who choose to be husbands of unchaste women belonging to a lower order of life and lead like brutes a life of shamelessness, fall after death into a pit of hell, a sea of pus, refuse, urine, phlegm and swallow the same most detestable things

Those Brahmins and others who act like husbands of bitches and asses and find delight in chasing animals and killing them in violation of Sastra are after death made the target and pierced with the arrows of merciless beings

Those men who mercilessly slaughtei animals are born as animals in the Hell of slaughter-house, and are dealt with in a similar manner

Those sinful twice-born men who deluded by passion cause their wives born of the same blood (Gotra) drink their semen, are thrown into a sea of semen and made to drink it

Those who set fire to others' houses and administer poison to others oi plunder villages and caravans —be they kings or kings' employees—they fall after death into a hell where they are voraciously munched by seven hundred and twenty hounds, with their dreadful teeth

Who utters falsehood in giving evidence or in making gifts, falls into a hell called Avichimat where there is no support to stand upon There the Jiva is hurled headlong from the summit of peaks of mountains four hundred miles in height In this hell even hard stony surface appears like water and thus the Jiva is made to delude himself ever more Though his body is shattered to pieces he does not die, and he is repeatedly lifted up to the top and hurled down again and again

If a Brahmin drinks wine or eats objectionable food, he is made to drink molten iron in the region of hell Those who go against the prescribed rules of Varnashrama Dharma are given suitable punishments here

Those men who praise themselves as great personages, but do not respect those who are really great by birth honour and learning, are truly living corpses and after death are thrown head foremost into a hell of brinish mire to undergo endless torments

Those who worship gods by offering human victims, are thrown into a hell where they are cut to slices and eaten by devils, but even then they do not die but only experience pain

Those wicked people who torment their refugees —because they are under their control—are made after death to suffer from extreme hunger and thirst and are on every side assailed by sharp instruments, and are made to recollect their sins

Those who are here cruel like snakes by nature and terrify other beings, fall when they die, into a hell called Dandasuka, where snakes of five or seven hoods attack them and worry them to death even though they do not die

Those who here imprison people in dark holes and dungeons are in turn after their death imprisoned in dark atmosphere filled with fire and smoke

The eyes of those householders who get angry with guests and look at them with cruel eyes, as if they would burn them, are plucked out after death by vultures possessing bills hard like adamantine rock

He who having possessed much wealth, constantly suspects others as being thieves, and always watches over his treasure like a devil with a restless mind, becomes a devil in a waterless hell filled with darkness and filth He falls into a hell called Suchimukha

There are hundreds and thousands of such hells, which cannot be easily described here They are only specimens of such hells for suffering sinners and transgressors of law

Those who control their senses, who lead the path of Nivritti, who absorb themselves in Divine Meditation, who are good, kind and generous, who care a naught for this sensuous earth, who are intent on Supreme Moksha, are liberated beyond embodiment Virtuous people get the joyous heaven for enjoyment Others fall into one or the other of these hells, in case they are not born again on this earth

(From the Srimad Bhagavata)

Asurya Loka

Hell is a state of absolute and complete separation from the Lord, wherein man is not feeling the light of His love, Holiness and Truth There is no illumination It is a Sunless world—Asurya Loka All is chaos, darkness and torment due to the reaction and retribution of sin that has been wilfully, perversely and unrepentantly done.

There is no such thing as eternal damnation or eternal hell-fire for the sinners It cannot be It is a theory that has long been exploded. Eternal damnation is an ungodly doctrine, a terror and nightmare for ages To make people desist from doing wicked actions a terrifying description of hell is given It is Bhayanaka Shabda

God has not created men to become everlasting fuel to feed the flame of Hell. This is not certainly

His purpose in His creation If God be such, no one will pay homage to Him Who then can be saved? How many spotless men are there in this world? Who is of such untainted character as to receive a direct passport to heaven?

Even Pundits, Sastris Acharyas, priests, religious preachers Popes, Bishops and Archbishops, almost the whole population of this world will be roasted in hell-fire

The Way to Yama Loka

Two fierce messengers of Death stand before the lowest and the worst sinner with frightful looks The sinner is bound by the noose thrown by the messen engers Stricken by terror he passes urine He is endowed with a special thick body called 'Yatana Deha' to undergo the sufferings on the path The messengers bind him with chords and forcibly drag him along distant routes to the city of Samyamani

There is no shade of trees on the way There is neither food, nor water Twelve suns blaze The sinful soul goes along, pierced sometimes by cold winds, in one place torn by thorns, in another stung by very venomous serpents and scorpions He is burnt by fire in another place

With a broken heart, and the threats of a cruel guide shivering with fear, bitten by merciless hounds, conscious of his past sins, tortured by hunger and thirst, burnt by the fierce sun, marching through red-hot sand and severely beaten on the back though half falling down in a swoon, he is made to rise again and carried to the abode of Lord of Death He is condemned to prolonged sufferings and passing through gradations of grossest of animal lives, in the process of evolution like pigs and dogs, he attains gradually a human body after a process of purification of such sufferings

In one place he falls into a hidden well, in another from a lofty mountain, in another he treads on razor edges and on spear-points In one place he stumbles in the awful blackness and falls into water, in another in mud abounding in leeches, in another in hot slime In another place is a plain of hot sand made of smelted copper, in another a mound of embers In some places are showers of charcoal, showers of stones and thunderbolts, showers of blood, showers of weapons, showers of boiling water

In the midst of the way flows the terribly horrible Vaitarani river with pus, blood. It is difficult to cross this river

The sinner is beaten with hammers by the terrible messengers of Yama He is forcibly dragged by the nooses He eats the monthly rice-balls given by his sons If the son makes a gift of a cow the departed soul gets a boat to cross the Vaitarani river

He reaches the abode of Yama at the end of a year Lord Yama asks Chitragupta about the sins Chitragupta enquires of the Sravanis who are the sons of Brahma, who know all about the actions of the human beings The Sravanis, wives of the Sravanas, know accurately all that is done by women Earth, water, fire, air, ether (sky), the heart. Yama, day and night, the two twilights, justice the sun and moon know the actions of man

Lord Yama, the king of justice, gives fitting punishment to the sinners Then the cruel messengers take them to hell and torture them Again and again the messengers beat the sinners with spears, maces and pestles

The virtuous are wafted in heavenly cars to the gardens of Paradise which they gain by their virtuous acts in life But the highly sinful soul meets with icebergs and caverns strewn with thorn and pointed steel pikes, and bushes and shrubs on its way, as the punishment for its sins

Those of the mediocre class, have a clear and fine passage, with soft grassy path-ways strewn with cooling arbours and supplied with spring waters on both their sides

On its arrival there, the soul reflects within itself thus "Here am I and yonder is Yama, the Lord of death That other is the judge of our actions, Chitragupta, and this, his judgment given on my behalf"

Here in Yama's court, the judgment is pronounced for the Jiva, so that it might reap the reward of its acts, whereby it ascends either to the blissful heaven above or descends to the painful hell below

After having enjoyed the pleasures of Svarga or suffered the pains of hell, it is doomed to return to this earth again to undergo the result of its acts in repeated births.- This is the significance of the periodical ceremonies done for the deceased, for the first one year after a man's death

The City of Justice

Lord Yama is the King of justice His city is built of diamonds and jewels It is effulgent and impregnable It is full of palaces and mansions It has four gateways It is surrounded by high ramparts It measures a thousand Yojanas Chitragupta, the recorder of fate of all human beings, also dwells in this city of Justice He records the good and evil of men This marvellous city was created by the architect of the universe by the power of his Yoga There is a divine assembly place All those assembled are knowers of the Scriptures All are devoted to righteousness The Royal sages also are there The sinners who go by the southern part do not behold it Those who go into the mansion of righteousness by the three gateways, eastern and others, are men of virtuous actions

There is an eastern way covered with the stalks of Parijata trees and paved with jewels The holy Brahmins, sages, the royal sages, the devotees of Lord Siva, those who build rest houses, who give shelter to the ascetics during the rainy season, those who are free from anger and greed, those who delight in truth and righteousness, those who delight in the service of their teachers, those who make gifts of land, houses and cows, those who tell and listen to the sacred Scriptures, are travellers on this path They go to the assembly of Righteousness

The second, the northern way, is paved with yellow sandalwood There is a pleasant tank full of the essence of nectar Those who are learned in the Vedas who honour guests, who are worshippers of Durga and the Sun, those who die for the sake of Brahmins, in the service of the master, those who die in the protection of cattle, those who delight in making great gifts, enter the northern gate and reach the assembly of Righteousness

The third, the western way, is beautified with jewelled mansions Those who are devoted to Lord Vishnu and Lakshmi, those who repeat the Gayatri Mantra, those who maintain household fires, those who repeat the Vedas, those who are endowed with dispassion those who perform the five sacrifices those who perform Sraddha for the forefathers, those who perform the Sandhya at the proper times, those who observe the vow of celibacy, those who turn away from injury to others, those who are faithful to their wives, those who are intent on the welfare of all beings, ascend the best of chariots, drink the nectar and enter the assembly of Righteousness by entering the western gate

Lord Yama welcomes them and honours them with sandal paste and other things They live there for some ages and enjoy superhuman happiness Then they take a holy human birth when their merits of good actions have been exhausted

Yama Sabha

The assembly-hall of Yama, the son of Vivaswan was built by Vishwakarma That effulgent Sabha covers an area of one hundred Yojanas It has the splendour of the Sun, it yields everything that one may desire to have from it. It is neither very cold nor very hot. It delights the heart

There is no grief, and no decrepitude, no hunger, no thirst, nor there is anything disagreeable, nor there is any kind of wretchedness or distress There can be no fatigue or any kind of evil-feelings in that Sabha Every object of desire, celestial or human is to be found in that hall, all kinds of enjoyable articles, as also sweet, juicy, agreeable and delicious things that are lickable, suckable or drinkable are all there in profusion The garlands that are there are of the most delicate fragrance and the trees that stand (around it) yield whatever fruits are desired

There are both cold and hot waters,—they are all sweet and agreeable There sit holy royal sages and stainless Brahmana Rishis They all cheerfully wait upon Yama—the royal sage Trasadasyu, Kritavirja, Srutasrava, Dhruva, etc —one hundred kings of the Martya race, one hundred of Nepa, and one hundred of the Huya race, one hundred kings of the name of Dhritarashtra, eighty of the name of Janamejaya, one hundred of the name of Brahmadatta, one hundred of the name of Iri and Ari, two hundred Bhishmas, one hundred Bhimas, one hundred Prativindas one hundred Nagas and one hundred Hayas

These holy royal sages, all of great achievements and great knowledge of the Shastras, wait upon Yama in that assembly-hall Agastha Malanga, Kala, the performers of sacrifices, the Sandhyas, Yogins, the living Pitris, the wheel of Time, the illustrious conveyor of sacrificial Ghee (Agni), all sinful men and those that died during winter solstice, those officers of Yama who have been appointed to count the allotted days of everybody and everything, Kasa and Kusha trees and all plants in their spiritual form wait upon Yama These and many others are the members of the assembly-hall of Yama They are so numerous to be mentioned here The Sabha is capable of going everywhere at will, it is wide of extent it is beautiful Vishwakarma has built it after long continued asceticism It is resplendent with its own effulgence It is visited by the ascetics of severe penances, of excellent vows, of truthful speech of pure and peaceful mind, and of heart sanctified by holy deeds,—all of shining bodies and all attired in spotless robes, all adorned in bracelets and garlands, and with their own holy acts and with the marks of their orders

Many illustrious Gandharvas and many Apsaras fill all parts of it with both instrumental and vocal music, and with sounds of dance and laughter Sacred perfumes and sweet sounds and the celestial garlands are all there in crowds Hundreds of thousands of virtuous men of celestial beauty and great wisdom always wait upon and worship the illustrious lord of all created beings

Indra Loka

The celestial Sabha of Shakra (Indra) is full of lustre and it was obtained by him as the fruit of his actions It was made by Indra himself as effulgent as the Sun Its breadth is one hundred Yojanas, its length is one hundred and fifty Yojanas it is five Yojanas in height. It can go anywhere at will

It dispels decripitude, grief, fatigue and fear, it is beneficial and auspicious, it is furnished with rooms and seats, it is charming and adorned with celestial trees In that Sabha sits on an excellent seat, the lord of the celestials with his wife Sachi, who is the embodiment of beauty and wealth With an indescribable vague form, with a crown on his head, with white bracelets on the upper arms, attired in pure white robes, and adorned with many coloured garlands, he sits there with Beauty Fame and Glory by his side

There daily wait upon that illustrious deity of one thousand sacrifices (Indra), all the Marutas—that lead the life of householders, the Siddhas, the celestial Rishis, the Sandhyas, the celestials, and the bright complexioned Marutas adorned with golden garlands These with their followers all possessing celestial forms and adorned with ornaments always wait upon and worship the illustrious chastiser of foes, the lord of the celestials

There wait upon Indra all the celestial Rishis of pure soul, all as effulgent as the fire, and all whose sins are completely washed off, all that are energetic, without grief of any kind, and without any fear (or anxiety),—all performers of Soma sacrifice, Parasara, Parvata, Savarni, Durvasa, Yajnavalkya, Uddalaka, etc Some of them are born of women, some not born of women,—some living on air, some on fire These Rishis worship the wielder of thunder (Indra), the Lord of all the worlds Sahadeva, Sunita, Samika,

Hiranmaya, Garga, etc and the celestial waters and plants, faith, intelligence and the goddess of learning Dharma, Artha, and Kama also lightning, clouds charged with rains, the winds, all the loud-sounding forces of heaven, the eastern point, the twenty-seven fires conveying the sacrificial Ghee, Agni Soma, the fire of Indra, Mitra, Savitri and Aryama, Bhaga, Sukra, the planets, the stars, the Mantras which are uttered in sacrifices, all these are present there.

Many charming Apsaras and Gandharvas gratify there the lord of the celestials with their various kinds of dances and vocal and instrumental music and with the exhibition of many skilful feats The Brahmana Rishis, all the royal and celestial sages adorned with garlands and ornaments often come to and go from that celestial assembly-hall riding on various kinds of celestial cars

Brihaspati and Shukra are always present there on all occasions These and many other illustrious Rishis of rigid vows, Bhrigu and the seven Rishis who are equal to Brahma himself, use always to come to and go from that assembly-hall, riding on cars as beautiful as the car of Soma This Sabha is named Pushkaramalini

Varuna Loka

The celestial Sabha of Varuna is matchless It dimension is exactly like that of Yama It is adorned with white walls and arches It is built by Viswakarma under the waters; it is surrounded on all side by many celestial trees made of gems and jewels an producing excellent fruits and flowers. Many plant with blue, yellow, black, white and red blossoms have formed themselves into excellent bowers Hundreds and thousands of beautiful and variegated birds of various species always pour forth their melodies within them.

That Sabha is very delightful; it is neither cold nor hot It is ruled by Varuna, and it consists of many rooms furnished with many charming seats Here sits Varuna with his queen (Varuni) adorned with celestial ornaments and jewels. Adorned with celestial garlands, perfumed with celestial scents and besmeared with paste of celestial fragrance, the Adityas wait there upon the lord of waters, Varuna

Vasuki, Takshaka, Janamejaya, etc, all having auspicious marks and Mandalas and broad hoods, wait upon Varuna, without any anxiety. The son of Virochana, Vali, Sangrodha those Danavas called Kalakpanja Suhanu, Pithara Dasagriva, all adorned with ear-rings, floral garlands and crowns and attired in celestial robes, all blessed with boons and possessed of great bravery and immortality, all well-conducted and of excellent vows, wait upon Varuna, the wielder of the noose (as his weapon) There wait upon him the four oceans, he rivers Bhagirathi, the Kalindi, the Vidisa, the Vnwa, the rapid Narmada, the Chandrabhaga, the Saraswati, the Iravati, the Sindhu, the Godavari, the Krishna, the Kaveri, the great Sone, the Sarayu, he red Mahanadi, the Gomati, etc, all other rivers, sacred Tirthas, lakes, wells, springs, tanks, large and small, all in their personified forms, the points of heavens, the earth, all the mountains, every specie c aquatic animals, wait upon the illustrious Varuna The Gandharvas and Apsaras, experts in vocal and instrumental music, wait upon Varuna, singing his eulogistic songs. All the charming mountains, that are rich in jewels, are present there engaged in sweet conversation. Varuna's minister, named Sunava, surrounded by his sons and grandsons, wait upon him along with the Pushkara Tirtha, called 'Go'. All these in their personified forms worship Varuna.

Kubera Loka

The greatly effulgent assembly-hall of Vaisravana (Kubera) is one hundred Yojanas in length and seventy Yojanas in breadth. It was built by Kubera himself by his ascetic powers. It is like the peak of Kailasa (mountain) and it outshines the brilliancy of the moon herself. Being supported by the Guhyakas, it looks as if it is attached to the firmament. Being adorned with celestial-made large palaces of gold, it displays great beauty.

It is extremely delightful and rendered fragrant with celestial perfumes. It is ornamented with many great jewels. Resembling the peaks of a mass of white clouds it seems to float in the sky. It is painted with colours of celestial gold, and therefore it appears as if it is adorned with streaks of lightning. Here sits on an excellent seat, which is as bright as the sun and which is covered with celestial carpets and furnished with beautiful footstools, the handsome king Vaisravana attired in excellent robes and adorned with costly ornaments and brilliant earrings, and surrounded by his one thousand wives.

Delicious and cool breezes blowing through the generous forests of Mandaras and carrying the fragrance of the field of Jasmine and also of the lotuses on the breast of the Alaka (the celestial river) and of the gardens of Nandana (the celestial wood) wait upon Kubera

There sing the celestials with the Gandharvas surrounded by various tribes of Apsaras in notes of celestial sweetness Misrakeshi, Rambha, Urvasi, Lata, and a thousand other Apsaras and Gandharvas all great experts in music and dance wait upon the lord of wealth That assembly-hall filled with the notes of instrumental and vocal music and with the sounds of various Gandharvas and Apsaras is extremely charming and delicious

The Gandharvas named Kinnaras and others, Hamsachura, Vrikshavaspa and many other Yakshas by hundreds and thousands always wait upon Kubera The illustrious Lakshmi and also Nala Kubera always remain there (in that Sabha) Many others often go there Many Brahmana Rishis and celestial Rishis always go there, many Rakshasas and Gandharvas wait there There wait upon his friend, the lord of wealth, being ever cheerful and knowing no fatigue, the illustrious (deity), the husband of Uma, the Lord of all creatures, the three-eyed God, accompanied by his wife and surrounded by innumerable spirits, some of dwarfish stature, some of fearful face, some with blood-red eyes,—some feeding upon fat and flesh, and all armed with various weapons and possessed of the speed of wind

With cheerful heart hundreds of Gandharva chiefs attired in their respective robes worship Kubera The chief of the Vidvadharas, Chakradhamana with his followers wait upon Kubera Many Kinnaras, innumerable kings with Bhagdatta at their head and the chief of Kimpurushas Druma, the chief of the Rakshasas, Mahendra, all wait upon Kubera

The virtuous Vivishana waits upon his elder brother Kubera The (mountains) Himalayas, Paripatra, Vindhya, Kailasha, Sunava, and many other in their personified forms with Meru at their head wait upon Kubera

The illustrious Nandiswara Mahakala, many spirits with arrowy ears and sharp pointed mouths and the deep-roaring white bull of Shiva, many other Rakshasas and Pishachas wait upon Kubera The son of Kubera surrounded by his attendants, always with his permission formerly used to worship by bowing his head to Shiva, the creator of the three worlds One day the high-souled Bhava (Shiva) made friendship with Kubera, and from that day he is always present in the assembly-hall of Kubera. Those princes of all wealth, Sankha and Padma (in their personified forms) accompanied by gems, wait upon the lord of wealth

The assembly-hall of Kubera is capable of moving in the firmament.

Goloka

Kine form the support of all creatures Kine are the refuge of all creatures Kine are the embodiments of virtue Kine are sacred and kine are purifiers of all. They have excellent forms and qualities

Kine form high and excellent energy. The gift of kine is highly spoken of Those good men, who, shorn of pride, make gift of kine, are considered as doers of righteous deeds and as givers of all articles Such men acquire the highly sacred region of kine

The trees there yield sweet fruits Indeed, those trees are always bedecked with excellent flowers and fruits. Those flowers have celestial fragrance

The entire soil of that region is formed of gems The sands there are all gold The climate there possesses the excellences of every season There is no mire, no dust It is indeed highly sacred

The rivers there shine in resplendence for the red lotuses blossoming upon their bosoms, and for the jewels, gems and gold that are on their banks and which display the effulgence of the morning Sun.

There are many lakes also on whose breasts are many lotuses, mixed here and there with *Nymphaea stellata,* and having their petals made of costly gems and their filaments gold-hued

They are also bedecked with flowering forests of the *Nerium odorum* with thousands of beautiful creepers twining round them, as also with forests of Santanakas bearing flowers

There are rivers whose banks are variegated with many bright pearls and shining gems and gold

Parts of those regions are covered with excellent trees that are decked with jewels and gems of every sort. Some of them are made of gold and some of them are effulgent like fire.

There stand many mountains made of gold, and many hills made of jewels and gems These shine in beauty on account of their tall summits made of all sorts of gems

The trees that bedeck those regions always put forth flowers and fruits, and are always covered with dense foliage The flowers always yield a celestial fragrance and the fruits are greatly sweet

The righteous persons always sport there happily Freed from grief and anger, they spend their time there, crowned with the fruition of every desire

Pious and illustrious persons sport there happily, moving from place to place in delightful and highly beautiful cars

Bevies of celestial nymphs always amuse there with music and dance Indeed a person goes to such regions as the fruit of his making gifts of kine

Those regions which are owned by Pushan, and the Marutas of great power, are acquired by givers of kine In riches the royal Varuna is considered as pre-eminent The giver of kine acquires riches like that of Varuna himself

He who serves kine with respect and who follows them with humility, succeeds in getting many invaluable boons from kine which become pleased with him

One should never, even in his heart, injure kine. One should, indeed, always confer happiness on them. One should always respect kine and adore them by bending low his head.

In Vaikuntha all persons dwell having the form of Vishnu and propitiate Him by means of Dharma which is not prompted by the desire of any fruit.

There dwells the glorious First Person who is only in the range of words (who is to be known only by the Vedanta) who having associated Himself with the Sattva unmixed with Rajas, showers blessings on us His devotees, whom He would make happy

There stands a garden called "The Highest Happiness" filled with trees that yield all that is desired and it shines like the embodiment of the final beatitude

In that Vaikuntha-loka the Muktas that move about in Vimanas along with their consorts are indifferent to the perfumed breeze, though their mind is agitated by the fragrance of the Madhavi flowers (creepers) dripping with honey in the middle of water, and they always sing the Lord's deeds which cleanse the world of all sin

Vaikuntha Loka

In Vaikuntha, while the kingly bee hums as if singing the story of Hari, there comes for a moment a lull in the tumult of pigeons, cuckoos, cranes, the ruddy geese, Chatakas swans, parrots, Tittiris and peacocks

There the Mandara, the Kunda, the Kurava, the Utpala, the Champaka, the Arna, the Punnaga, the Naga, the Bakula, the Ambuja, and the Parijata, all these flowers endowed with fragrance as they are, regard very highly the Tapas of Tulasi when her fragrance is appreciated and valued by Hari who wears the garland of Tulasi as His ornament

That Vaikuntha Loka is thronged with Vimanas of Vaidurya (cat's eyes), emerald and gold, which are visible only to those that bow at His feet, and there women of stout hips and smiling faces do not, by their maddening smiles and other arts, excite the passion of those Muktas who have given their hearts to Krishna

There, in the abode of Hari, the faultless Goddess Lakshmi in a beautiful form, with her arms freely suspended, with lotus-like feet resounding with anklets, appears by her image reflected on the crystal walls chased with gold, as if engaged in dusting the house—Lakshmi whose grace is sought after by others (Brahma and all others)

There, in her own garden, and at the wells of pure nectar-like waters surrounded by parapets of coral, while worshipping the Lord with Tulasi, Lakshmi saw her own face with beautiful looks and prominent nose reflected on the water and thought that it was kissed by the glorious Lord

To that Vishnu-loka do not go those, who listen to bad stories which spoil the mind, because they concern subjects other than the deeds (creation etc) of Hari who shatters the sin of His devotees. The bad stories, which when heard by unfortunate men, deprive them of all merit and alas! throw them into hells of darkness where no relief is possible.

These are men, who deluded by the widespread Maya, do not perform the worship of this most gracious Lord, though they have attained this human life which is sought after even by us and in which it is possible to gain the knowledge of truth along with the practice of Dharma

Thither go those men who are far above us and possessed of enviable virtue and character, men from whom Yama stands aloof, (or who have risen above Yama, Niyama and other restrictions), on whose body the hair stand on end and from whose eyes tears flow, their mind and heart being overwhelmed by intense love in their mutual conversations about the Lord of delightful glories

Vaikuntha, the one region worthy of praise in all the worlds, which is shining most splendid with its most beautiful and wonderful mansions of the gods and wise men and which is in short a region of divine nature, is occupied by the Father of the universe

There are seven entrances to Vaikuntha In each entrance there are two gods of the same age armed with Gada, beautifully adorned with invaluable Keyura, Kundala and Kireeta, who wear about their necks and between their four blue arms, Vanamala (the so-called wreath) about which swarm gladsome bees, and who appear to wear a face somewhat dark with anger from the bent brow, the prominent nose (wide nostrils) and red eyes

The Seven Planes

There are seven planes They are Bhuloka (earth plane), Bhuvarloka (Antariksha or the astral plane), Svargaloka (heaven or the mental plane), Maharloka, Janarloka, Tapoloka and Satyaloka (Brahmaloka or the world of Brahma, the Creator) Tapasvins dwell in Tapoloka If you keep different kinds of lights in a room such as kerosene oil light, mustard oil light, petromax candle light, electric light, the various lights interpenetrate in the room Even so, the Lokas interpenetrate Each plane has its own matter of an appropriate degree of density, which interpenetrates the matter of the plane next below it.

The astral plane, or Bhuvarloka, interpenetrates the earth plane and extends for some distance beyond it The mental plane interpenetrates the astral but also extends further into space than does the latter The vibrations of the astral world are more rapid or quicker than those of the physical plane The vibrations of the mental plane are more rapid or quicker than those of the astral plane. The vibrations of the Satyaloka are more rapid or quicker than those of the mental plane In each plane the soul develops a new and higher sense of power

When you pass from one plane to another you do not move in space You simply change your consciousness You change your focus of consciousness. You can have different sorts of vision through the telescope or microscope by using lenses of different degrees of potency or power You have got different vehicles within yourself which correspond to different planes and which can function in different planes

In the dreaming-state your astral body functions. In the deep sleep state your causal body functions. Even so, in the astral plane your astral body operates, in the mental plane your mental body operates, in the Brahmaloka your causal body functions. Each plane is formed by matter of different degrees of density In the mental plane the matter is subtler than in the astral plane In the causal plane the matter is subtler than the matter of mental plane The planes occupy the same position in space Heaven is here Brahmaloka is here Have a different vehicle or body and a different subtler eye You can function in any plane

In the physical plane one gets knowledge of objects through the five Jnana Indriyas or organs of knowledge, viz., ear, skin, eye, tongue, nose In the mental plane or heaven he does not hear, see and feel by separate and finite organs He gets a Divya Chakshu or a divine eye, an extraordinary new power or faculty He can hear see, feel and know everything of an object instantaneously, through this new mental eye He gets an accurate and perfect knowledge of all objects He is not deceived or misled by any external appearance There is no misunderstanding

In the mind all the powers of all the senses are blended Mind is a mixture or compound of all the organs It can hear, see, taste, smell and feel

He can get everything by mere Sankalpa or willing. If he thinks of a celestial car, it is there before him at once If he thinks of a place, he is there immediately. If he thinks of a person, he is before him at once. There is no distance for him There is no feeling of separation for him He reads the thoughts of others Hence, questions and answers are not necessary in the mental plane. The interchange of ideas is very quick

He can know the past and the future also He is endowed with clairvoyance and clairaudience He can simultaneously manifest himself in various forms

Heaven is a plane of enjoyment only It is a place to reap the fruits of one's good Karmas done in the earth plane One cannot do fresh Karmas there He cannot attain Moksha or the final emancipation from there He will have to come down to this earth again for trying again for his salvation

Indra, Varuna, Agni, etc, are the original Devatas or gods of heaven There are Karma-Devas also here These are men who have raised themselves to the status of Devas through meritorious actions done in the earth plane A Deva has a Taijasic body. Fire preponderates The Devas exhibit different degrees of brilliance in accordance with different degrees of advancement

There is neither day nor night for a Deva or an inhabitant of the mental plane or heaven. He is neither sleeping nor waking When he enters heaven he experiences intense happiness This is his waking state He sinks into a state of unconsciousness when the term of life in heaven terminates

Brahmaloka is the world of Brahman or Hiranyagarbha This is also known by the name Satyaloka Those who go by the path of Devayana reach this plane Those who perform meritorious actions without expectation of fruits and who lead the life of purity and righteousness and those who worship Hiranyagarbha and all realized Bhaktas will go to this realm

They attain Krama-mukti or progressive emancipation They enjoy all the Divine Aiswaryas of the Lord and in the end of the cycle merge themselves in Para Brahman along with Brahma, the Creator

Brahmaloka becomes Vaikuntha or appears as Vaikuntha for a devotee of Lord Hari It becomes Kailasa or Shivaloka or appears as Shivaloka for a devotee of Lord Shiva It is the Bhav that works

The Stay on Supra-physical Planes

Interval Between Death and Rebirth

People wish to know the exact period that elapses from the time of leaving the body and being born again. Does the soul take a new body in one year? Does it take ten years? How long does one live upon the subtler planes before reappearing on the earth plane? These are some of the questions Now, there is no definite period of time in this matter In main two factors decide this issue viz, the nature of the individual Karma and the last impression before death It may vary from hundreds of years to a few months even Those that work out some of their Karmas in other planes in subtler regions, take a considerable time before entering a fresh body The interval is very long, for a year of the earth period passes off as a single day on the celestial plane There is an instance cited, where, seeing the amazement and admiration of foreign tourists at the imposing ruins of certain ancient monuments, a saint present in the vicinity remarked, that some of these very people have fashioned these monuments centuries ago Now they look in amazement upon their own handwork

A very sensual individual with strong craving or one with intense attachment sometimes is reborn quickly Also in cases where life is cut short by a violent death or a sudden unexpected accident, the Jiva resumes the thread very soon This was so in the case of the Amritsar girl, Mahindra Kumari She was reborn within 7 months of her death in October, 1939 So strong was her desire to see her brother at the time of death. Usually in such cases of immediate rebirth, the Jiva often remembers many of the events of its previous life It recognises its former relatives and friends and identifies old home and familiar objects. This sometimes leads to very queer developments. There are some instances where a murdered person, being reborn, has declared the manner of his death and revealed the identity of the killer in the recent past

Thus, for instance Dharmarajya reported (23-3-36) in a village in Gwalior, that a village Patwari offended one Thakur Chotey Lal by making some false entries in the village records prejudicial to the latter's interest To avenge the wrong the Thakur trapped the Patwari in an ambush, shot him in the chest and severed the fingers of his right hand. Some time later, a son was born to a person at a place 14 miles from the scene of murder The child had a gun shot mark in his chest with the fingers of the right hand missing When the child could speak, the father one day asked him if the Creator had forgotten to make the fingers The child at once replied that Chotey Lal Thakur had shot him in the chest and severed the fingers and gave details of the incident which were then verified.

A reincarnated individual had at times unerringly gone and uncovered the treasure that had been hidden away by him or her. In the vast majority this memory is not present This is really a blessing conferred by the all-wise Being Such recollection would greatly complicate our present lives The past is veiled to you until such time as it is good and helpful to remember it When you attain perfection and reach the end of a cycle, all will be revealed and you will see a whole rosary of lives threaded upon the one personality

But such cases of immediate rebirth are not common Generally for an average individual the interval between death and rebirth happens to be a considerable period measured in terms of earth time Persons who have done much good Karmas spend a great deal of time on the Daivic plane before being born again. Great souls, spiritually advanced persons, wait for a long time before reincarnating.

In the intervening period between death and new birth that departed spirit, specially if the person is psychically, and spiritually developed can frequently materialize upon the earth plane if necessity arises It takes human form, talks, and can even make itself felt by tangible touch It is possible to photograph such an apparition

Such materialised form is different from the astral body The latter is not visible to normal vision It is an exact counterpart, a subtle 'double' to the physical body and forms the vehicle in which the departed soul journeys after death

But, however, astral consciousness cannot guarantee you freedom from birth and death. Occultism and spiritualism can never give ultimate emancipation nor reveal the full secret of the beyond. Spiritual realisation and knowledge of the Self alone will reveal the mystery of Life and death, and the life beyond Death.

CHAPTER SEVEN

SPIRITUALISM

Spiritualism

Death is the most common phenomenon in nature and yet the least understood fact. It is one of the most difficult problems of philosophy, because there is no direct evidence usually available as to what really happens in and after death.

The practice of Yoga enables one to observe the phenomenon of death through the intuitive eye of wisdom or Divya Chakshu. Maharshi Vasishtha claims to have known everything directly and speaks on death upon his own experience.

Recently there has been an attempt made in the West by the Psychical Research Society to study the problem of death. Some thinkers have come to believe on the strength of the evidence collected that death does not bring human personality to an end.

Sir Oliver Lodge made scientific experiments. He is now convinced that there is the survival of life after death. He says:

"In justice to myself and my co-workers I must risk annoying my hearers not only by leaving on record our conviction that occurrences now regarded as occult can be examined and reduced to order by the methods of science carefully and persistently applied, but by going further and saying with the utmost brevity that already the facts so examined have convinced me, that memory and affection are not limited to that association with matter by which alone they can manifest themselves here and now, and that personality persists beyond death The evidence to my mind goes to prove that discarnate intelligence under certain conditions, may interact with us, on the material side thus indirectly coming with our scientific ken"

The modern tendency is to speculate more and more on the life after death, after the advent of spirit communications, table tiltings, spirit taps, spirit light, spirit-writings, slate writings, materialised hands card liftings, tin trumpeting, planchette writings, Ouija board manipulating and communications through media Articles are freely written on the subject both in the West and in the East There are many numbers of societies for the psychic research in the West The effect of those researches has been able to convince the West of the survival of the soul after death

The Westerner with the stage of ad- atheists.
vancement at which he has reached now
for scientific demonstration of every of foretel-
may find revelations and discoveries they have love
of the soul, through this phenomena relatives They
proofs and demonstrations. To this, misfortunes,
ern philosophy, bred and brought warning mes-
scriptures of India, the existence of

transmigrations are only the beginning of his philosophy To the West it has come to be almost the end of their researches till now

According to the spiritualistic school of thought the other world to which we go after death consisted of a number of spheres representing various shades of luminosity and happiness for which our spiritual conditions have fitted us In these spheres the scenery and conditions of this world were closely reproduced and so also was the general framework of society Death was made easy by presence of celestial beings who led the new comer into his existence

The souls of Jivanmuktas or great sages who have merged in the Absolute cannot by any amount of invocations, or spirit calls, or mediums, be recalled

A departed spirit may bear intense love tov its former relations and friends. It may communic with its survivors on earth

Dying persons have very strong attachment to their children. If there are no persons to take care of their children, they project their astral body after death, appear before the relatives and give a message There have been records of such cases

problem.
lieve on the departed souls who have intense attach-
death does not tives become earth-bound. They hover
n, remain close to them and try to help
Sir Oliver Lo y to be loved by them They are con-
is now convinced personality. They do not know that
after death He sa

"In justice to sitting in his room He is thinking of risk annoying moblem. He is alone in the room The room is closed He beholds his 'double' which is like him This comes out of him, goes to the table, takes a piece of paper and pencil in hand, solves his problem and writes the answer on the paper This double is the astral self of the man which can live independent of the gross physical body Such instances are recorded in the Psychical Research Society of Europe and America This clearly proves that there is a soul which is entirely distinct from the gross physical body

After death the individual soul takes all his desires with it and it creates the objects of enjoyment by mere thinking If it thinks of orange, the orange is there and it eats the orange If it thinks of tea, tea is there and it drinks tea

He who wants to drink wine in heaven and eat delicious fruits and to live with celestial damsels and move in celestial cars, goes to a plane of consciousness where he will project all these ideas and make his own heaven

Modern spiritualism has given wonderful demonstrations regarding the existence of disembodied spirits who continue to live even after the dissolution of their gross physical bodies This has opened the eyes of the rank materialists of the West and the atheists.

Some good spirits possess the powers of foretelling, clairvoyance and clairaudience They have love and affection for their friends and relatives They try to help them during their distress, misfortunes, dangers and calamities. They give a warning message to avert dangers

The disembodied spirits remain earth-bound for some time after their death They expect help from their relatives and friends Prayers, Kirtan, Sraddhas, charitable acts, good thoughts help the departed souls in getting release from the earth-bound conditions and rising higher and entering the world of Pitris in order to enjoy the fruits of their good deeds

The spirits have no knowledge of the highest truth They cannot help others in attaining Self-realisation Some are foolish, deceitful and ignorant These earth-bound spirits control the mediums and pretend to know everything regarding the planes beyond death They speak falsehood They put on the appearance of some other spirit and deceive the audience. The poor innocent mediums are not aware of the tricks played by their dishonest spirit-guides The spiritualists waste their time, energy and money in the vain hope of obtaining the favour of those spirits and transcendental knowledge through them

The last thoughts of the spiritualists will be thoughts of spirits only They cannot have sublime thoughts of God Hence they will enter the region of the spirits only Communication with the spirits will mar their onward march to higher blissful regions and make them earth-bound. Therefore, give up the idle curiosity of talking to the dead on everything regarding the spirit world You will not gain anything tangible and substantial You will disturb their peace

No one should allow himself to become a medium The mediums have lost the power of self-control Their vital energy, life-force and intellectual powers are used by the spirits which control them The mediums do not gain any higher divine knowledge These spirits are not angels as the spiritualists claim. They are really earth-bound spirits

The spirits do portrait-painting and typing Spirits materialise in the seance. They melt away in a mist-like white substance and disappear You can hear the noise of the pencil during automatic slate writing You may feel a gentle shock while the spirit writes in the slate The spirits may place their hands upon you and catch hold of your shirt, tie, etc

You create your destiny, your character, your future through your thoughts and deeds There is no end of your experiences here and hereafter You will continue to live and come back and be born again on this earth Try to attain perfection and reach that state where there is no more birth, no more death, and no more disease, sorrow, tribulation or suffering Meditate on the eternal Atman, thy innermost Self Do not identify yourself with this perishable body, a combination of the five elements Realise the Self and be free. Through knowledge of the Imperishable obtain perfect peace, eternal bliss, everlasting joy and immortality.

CHAPTER EIGHT

SHRADDHA AND PRAYER FOR THE DEAD

Importance of Shraddha Ceremony

The Karma Kanda of the Vedas, the sacred books of the Hindus, has laid down different duties of man according to his position in life and according to the order to which he belongs All these injunctions are embodied in the book called Manusmriti Manusmriti is the code of law and conduct for the Hindus Kings and rulers of the past were guided by the rules contained therein for the maintenance of peace and order in the country The Manusmriti has divided human society into four main divisions known as Brahmana, Kshatriya, Vaisya and Sudra It has also made four divisions of the different stages of life of an individual viz., Brahmacharya, Garhasthya, Vanaprastha and Sannyasa Brahmacharya is the life of a student, Garhasthya the household life, Vanaprastha the life in the forest given to religious pursuits and lastly Sannyasa, the life of a mendicant after renouncing all worldly activities These are the four Ashramas of life

This order of society gradually perished due to modern civilization and deterioration of spiritual life in man. Materialistic dark forces of Rajas and Tamas have overpowered the effects of Sattvic ones and religion is given secondary importance Nay, religionists are looked upon with contempt in these days A devotee or a Sadhak with a tuft of hair (Choti) is not liked by the modern men of the University Study of scriptures, observances of religious rites, a spiritual life of moderation and real ethical cultures are denounced as useless or old-fashioned and consequently they are fading into insignificance The problem of life is very serious now The struggle for existence is very keen in these days The question of food and other luxuries of life has taken the place of religion

For a householder the scriptures have imposed the Pancha Maha Yajnas the five great sacrifices obligatory duties of life The neglect of these duties entails penalty These great sacrifices are —1 Deva Yajna (sacrifice to Gods) 2 Rishi Yajna (sacrifice to Rishis) 3 Pitri Yajna (sacrifice to ancestors) 4 Bhuta Yajna (sacrifice to animals) and 5 Atithi Yajna (sacrifice to guests)

The Shraddha ceremony comes under Pitri Yajna It is the sacred duty of the householder Every householder should perform the Shraddha ceremony of his ancestors Pitris are forefathers who dwell in the Pitriloka They possess the powers of clairvoyance and clairaudience When Mantras are recited, they exercise tremendous influence through their vibrations The Pitris hear the sounds through the power of clairaudience and they are pleased They bless those who offer the oblation In Shraddha, the essence of food offerings is taken up by the Sun's rays to Suryaloka and the departed souls are pleased with the offerings Even in Germany and other foreign countries many persons perform Tarpan and Shraddha They have scientifically investigated the beneficial effects of such oblations It is the imperative duty of all householders to perform Shraddha and Tarpan to please the Rishis and Pitris Gita and the Upanishads clearly bear testimony to the fact that the performance of Shraddha is very important It is only the deluded souls with perverted intellect who misconstrue things and neglect to perform the sacred ceremonies and consequently suffer They are misguided by false reasoning and logic Satanic influences affect them very easily Ignorance is the root cause for this state of affairs

Shraddha ceremony is done once in every year A day of the Pitris is equal to one year of human computation This is the reason why we have to perform Shraddha ceremony once in a year If we perform Shraddha once in every year, it is equal to daily performances of Shraddha for the Pitris In their calculation we, their sons, live only for a few days, because the longest period of human existence of 100 years is merely 100 days for them

Some people entertain the doubt, "when the Jiva undergoes transmigration and takes another birth after leaving this physical body, is it necessary that we should perform Shraddha ceremony for him? He is no more in the heavens To whom will the oblations reach?" In the ninth chapter of the Gita, Lord Krishna has made it very clear that those virtuous persons who perform sacrifices for the attainment of heaven attain to those worlds of enjoyments. "They having enjoyed that spacious world of Svargas, their merit (Punya) exhausted, enter the world of the mortals, thus following the Dharma of the triad, desiring objects of desires, they attain to the state of going and returning" This establishes the theory of attainment of heaven after death, and rebirth in the mortal world after the exhaustion of virtuous acts The enjoyments in heaven and peace of the soul are enhanced by the performance of Shraddha ceremony The suffering in worlds other than heaven according to the merits of one's own actions is mitigated by the performance of Shraddha ceremony by his sons So in both cases the performance of Shraddha is a great help The Pitris remain in heaven (Pitriloka, Chandra Loka) for a very long period

According to the theory of transmigration, even if the individual is to take another birth immediately after his death, the performance of Shraddha adds to his happiness in his new birth So it is the imperative duty of everybody to perform Shraddha ceremony for his parents and forefathers Shraddha ceremony should be performed with great Shraddha (faith) as long as you live Faith is the main support for religion In olden days the question "whether to perform Shraddha ceremony or not" did not arise at all Then people were full of faith and had reverence for the scriptures In these days when faith is almost dwindling into an airy nothing and when the list of non-performers of Shraddha increased, others of wavering faith, begin to doubt whether it is necessary to perform Shraddha or not and whether any good will accrue out of it This lack of faith in the Shastras has degraded us to the present deplorable condition "Shraddhavan Labhate Jnanam the man of faith attains knowledge and thereby immortality and eternal peace" is the declaration of the Gita

Some people argue and say that if a man once performs Shraddha ceremony to his forefathers at Gaya and other places of religious importance, he need not do it every year thereafter This is not a general rule and does not apply to all It applies only in certain exceptional cases If people take shelter under this exception and discontinue Shraddha ceremony by once offering Pinda etc , at Gaya, they do so out of sheer ignorance They consider it merely a burden to perform Shraddha ceremony and avoid it They have not discharged their duties properly

The various religious observances imposed upon mankind by the Shastras tend to purify the ignorant man The goal of Karma Yoga is purification of the mind Shraddha ceremony, being one of the obligatory duties as per the injunctions of scriptures, also tends to purify the mind Besides this, the forefathers are also pleased and their good wishes and blessings tend to our material and spiritual growth

People who die without a son will suffer in the other worlds (This is, of course, not applicable in the case of Nitya Brahmacharins and spiritual aspirants who tread the spiritual path alone after renouncing all selfish desires and worldly enterprises) That is the reason why people adopt a son before their death for the due performance of Shraddha ceremonies after their death. The Gita also supports this view "Patanti Pitaro Hyesham Luptapindodakakriyah" their forefathers fall (down to hell) deprived of the offerings of Pinda (rice-ball) and water

But, if a man is religious-minded and if he has discrimination and dispassion, belief in the Shastras and the Vedas, if he has led a virtuous life till the end of his life, if he has devoted his last days in devotional practices, Japa, meditation study etc (even if he has no son) he will not have a fall He will surely enjoy perfect peace He will not be affected by the dark forces of ignorance He is free from base attractions of the world The Lord takes care of his progress He has got self-surrender and there is no fear of downfall He has mental purity All religious observations have Chitta Suddhi (purification of the mind) as their goal This he attains by virtue of his past Samskaras and virtuous life in previous incarnations

People of some communities in India spend money enormously and indiscriminately on Shraddha ceremony for show This is mere wastage Money should not be spent on luxury It is a delusion to think that the Pitris will get more peace by spending more money Money does not count for the ease of the Pitris, but the intensity of Bhav, with which the Shraddha is performed, counts

On such occasions the poor and deserving persons are to be fed sumptuously Their necessities of life should be attended to Study of scriptures should be done on such days The performer of the Shraddha ceremony should observe spiritual discipline like Japa, meditation, Mouna etc He should maintain strict Brahmacharya He should not spend his time in idle pursuits He should pray to God for the whole day. Recitation of appropriate Vedic hymns should be done The story of Nachiketas of the Upanishads should be studied The performer attains immortality.

Revive the Vedic religion Tread the path of Truth Perform Shraddha ceremony Shake off this slothfulness and indifference to the path of righteousness. Awake, arise ! Tap the right source Stick to your Varnashrama Dharma There is no greater sacrifice than performance of one's own duty Study Gita daily. Live in the world, but be out of it Assimilate the teachings of Gita This is the surest way to success in life as well as God-realisation

May you enjoy the bliss of the eternal. May you attain the Immortal and imperishable seat of Brahman by regular performance of your Swadharma (duty), singing Hari's names, serving the sick and the poor, following the path of righteousness, by regular study of the Vedas and meditation on the Supreme Self ! May the Lord guide you in your activities !

Prayer and Kirtan for the Dead

The prayers, good thoughts or good wishes and Kirtan become helpful to the departed souls They can be of invaluable assistance to the dead Prayers for the dead form an integral part of most of the religions The Catholic Church conducts prayers for the dead

Prayer acts on the principle of a radio station and broadcasts the waves of good thoughts just as the radio station broadcasts waves of sound

Prayer or Kirtan is a mighty force which helps the departed souls in their progress towards heaven and their quiet passage through the intermediate state

The departed souls remain in a state of swoon or unconsciousness immediately after death They cannot feel that they are detached from their previous gross material bodies Prayers, Kirtan and good thoughts from the relatives and friends can give real solace to the departed souls They create a potent vibration and an awakening in their stupefied condition of mind and bring back their veiled consciousness The souls begin to realise that they are not really in their gross material bodies

Then they endeavour to cross the borderland, a narrow river of ether, which is known as Vaitarani by the Hindus Chinavat bridge by the Parsis and Sirat by the Mohammedans

The weeping and mourning and the uncontrolled grief of their relatives give them pains and drag them down from their astral planes This may seriously retard them on their way to the heaven-world This produces serious injury to them. When they are sinking peacefully and when they are ready to have glorious awakening in heaven, they are aroused into vivid remembrance of the mundane life by the weeping and wailing of their friends and relatives Their thoughts produce similar vibrations in their minds and produce acute pain and discomfort.

Therefore, relatives and friends should do Kirtan and prayers for the peace of the departed souls Then only they can really help and comfort them If ten or twelve persons sit together and do Kirtan and prayer, it will be decidedly more powerful and effective. Collective prayer and Kirtan exercise a tremendous influence

Why Scriptures are Read to a Dying Man?

Man takes birth in this world with a definite purpose It is not for mere sensual enjoyment that man is born in this world The goal of life is self-realisation or God-consciousness The various activities of life should ultimately lead to that ideal or goal, or else the life is wasted There is no difference between the life of a beast and that of a man if he does not attempt to attain the goal of life

In the Gita you will find "Whosoever leaving the body goes forth remembering Me alone, at the time of death, he attains My being, there is no doubt about this"

It is very difficult to keep up God-consciousness at the time of death when diseases torment the body when consciousness fades away Some people imagine "Why should a man become a Sadhu and spend his life in the Himalayas What is wanted is that one should think of God at the time of death That can be done even at home' This is a mistake

The thought of God comes to a man at the time of death only through the grace of the Lord You have to keep the practice of remembrance or Nama Smaran every day, every hour, rather every second When a strong habit is formed by unceasing practice throughout the period of your life, then it would be easy to remember God at the time of death For this you will have to lead a well-regulated life after learning it from a saintly personality and living with him for some years If you can do this while remaining in the world, it is all the more helpful for your spiritual growth You can be in the world and at the same time be out of it

Pursuing the worldly activities throughout the day and sleeping at night, you will find no time to think of God at all Even if you do some Japa or prayer for 10 or 15 minutes daily while the rest of the time you spend in worldly activities, you cannot make very great spiritual advancement Therefore, the remembrance of God should be constant so that the thought of God may come automatically at the time of death as well

A devotee says to the Lord "O Lord let me enter the cool shade of your lotus-like feet this very day when my senses are strong, when my memory is good When the intellect is perturbed and perverted at the time of death it may be carried away by the threefold diseases of the body" Even the most devout aspirant may fail to think of the Lord at the time of death due to the weakness of the physical body

That is the reason why Gita Bhagavata, Vishnu Sahasranama and other holy scriptures are recited at the death bed of the sick man even though he may not be able to speak he may hear what is read out to him This will help the sick man in forgetting the body idea or his ailment and think of the Lord. Man always desires to die a peaceful death with his mind fixed on God When his memory fails, these sacred sentences of the scriptures will remind him of his real nature

Ordinarily a dying man is haunted by various horrible thoughts He cannot concentrate his mind on God His mind will be clouded with innumerable thoughts He will be thinking. "Who will look after my young wife and children if I die? What will become of my property? Who will realise the outstanding dues from the debtors? I have not done such and such work The second son is not married The first son has not been blessed with a child The work is half finished, many law suits are pending judgment" Thus reviewing the actions of his whole life and thinking of the future he will feel miserable.

When holy books are read and if his interest in the Lilas of the Lord is created, there is every possibility of the man forgetting his worldly attachments The relatives gathered round him should not begin to weep Then his mind will be more afflicted On the other hand they must encourage him to think of God alone When the mind of the sick man is thus gradually turned from the network of worldly matters and centred on the picture or Lilas or teachings of the Lord, all favourable conditions are created thereby for the passing off of the life-breath The mind also is peacefully alighted on the thought of God

He will then repent for his follies and pray to God sincerely Sincere prayers can undo the evil effect of bad Karma Viveka and Vairagya will dawn in him in the twinkling of an eye Even if at the time of death, real Viveka and Vairagya dawn in him, it is enough to give him the solace which the soul strives for

Ajamila was a pious man, but due to contact with a woman of ill-fame in the forest he lost all his Tejas, divine splendour and Tapas Shakti When he saw the messengers of Yama threatening him with noose and spears, he called for Narayana, his second son As soon as he uttered the name of Narayana, the messengers of Vishnu arrived with the celestial car, drove away the messengers of Yama and took Ajamila to Vaikuntha

King Parikshit heard Srimad Bhagavata from Sri Suka, the born Siddha and the son of Sage Vyasa, for seven days He observed fast for seven days and on the seventh day Sri Suka initiated him into Brahma Vidya He meditated on the Supreme Tattwa and became one with Supreme Brahman The mighty Takshaka appeared before him and by his deadly venom killed Parikshit Parikshit felt as if some insect was licking his feet He went above body-consciousness He burnt his body by the fire of Yoga practice even before Takshaka bit him

King Khatwanga realised the Supreme Brahman in one hour

These great men had done intense Sadhana throughout life and they remembered the Lord constantly

May all realise God in this very birth by constant remembrance of Him ! May He appear before you at the time of your departure from this body

CHAPTER NINE

CONQUEST OF DEATH

Conquest of Death

All are terribly afraid of death No one wants to die Even intellectual persons who have grasped the idea that the Soul is Immortal and is distinct from the body are also awfully afraid of death. Mysterious is Moha or infatuated love for the body ! Mysterious is Maya or Avidya

This body is an instrument for all sorts of sensual enjoyments That is the reason why man is intensely attached to the body Through ignorance he identifies himself with the body Through erroneous misconception he has mistaken the impure, insentient, non-permanent, pain-giving body for the pure, sentient eternal, all-blissful Soul So he is caught up in the whirlpool of birth and death Man has lost his power of discrimination through the force of Avidya or ignorance From Avidya is born non-discrimination or Aviveka Hence he is not able to discriminate between the eternal and the non-eternal real and the unreal, Atma and Anatma, truth and falsehood, matter and the spirit, Jada and Chaitanya From Avidya is born egoism or the self-assertive principle Wherever there is egoism, there is play of the two currents Raga-dvesha or likes and dislikes He performs actions through likes and dislikes He takes bodies to reap the fruits of his actions Therefore, Avidya is the root-cause of human sufferings Avidya is the cause for Karmas and births If you free yourself from Avidya, through knowledge of the Imperishable Atman you will have conquest over death and merge yourself in the Immortal Sat-Chit-Ananda Brahman or the Absolute

The student of Jnana-Yoga equips himself with the four means of Salvation or Sadhana Chatushtaya, viz, Viveka, Vairagya (dispassion), Shad-sampat or sixfold virtues and Mumukshutva or intense yearning for the final emancipation Then he approaches a Brahma-srotri, Brahma-nishtha Guru, hears the Srutis or the Upanishads, then reflects on what he has heard, meditates constantly on Nirguna Brahman and attains Self-realisation or Atma-sakshatkara and thus achieves conquest of death

The student of Bhakti Yoga develops the Navavidha Bhakti or nine modes of devotion He does Japa of Mantra, does Kirtan and serves the devotees He does total ungrudging self-surrender to the Lord. He says to the lord, "I am Thine All is Thine Thy will be done" He attains the vision of the Lord and thus obtains mastery over death

The student of Raja Yoga practises Yama or self-restraint and Niyama or religious observances He sits, restrains the breath, withdraws the senses, controls the thoughts, practises Dharana (concentration), Dhyana (meditation) and Samadhi (union with the Lord) and thus attains conquest over death

The student of Hatha Yoga awakens the Kundalini Shakti, that is lying dormant in the Muladhara Chakra through Asanas, Pranayama, Bandhas and Mudras, takes it through different Chakras, viz, Swadhisthana, Manipuraka, Anahata, Vishuddha, Ajna and unites the Shakti with Lord Siva in the Sahasrara Chakra and thus attains conquest of death

A Karma Yogi purifies the heart through constant selfless service He kills egoism through self-sacrifice, attains illumination and thus achieves conquest of self

What is Death and How to Conquer It

Death is only a change of form. Death is only separation of the astral body from the physical body Why are you so much afraid of death, my dear Viswanathan?

Birth follows death just as waking follows sleep You will again resume the work that was left off by you in your previous life Therefore, do not be afraid of death

The idea of death has ever been the strongest motive power of religion and religious life Man is afraid of death In old age he tries to think of God If he remembers God even from his boyhood, he will reap a rich spiritual harvest in old age Man does not want to die He wants to live for ever This is the starting point of philosophy Philosophy enquires and investigates It boldly proclaims: "O man, do not be afraid of death There is an immortal abode That is Brahman. That is your own Atman that dwells in the chambers of your heart Purify your heart and meditate on this pure, immortal, changeless Self You will attain immortality"

O man, do not be afraid of death at all thou art immortal Death is not the opposite of life. It is only a phase of life Life flows on ceaselessly The fruit perishes but the seed is full of life The seed dies but a huge tree grows out of the seed The tree perishes but it becomes coal which has a rich life Water disappears but it becomes the invisible steam which contains the seed of a new life The stone disappears but it becomes lime which is full of new life The physical sheath only is thrown but life persists.

Can you tell me, friend, "is there anyone on the surface of this earth who is not afraid of death? Is there anyone who is not uttering the name of the Lord when he is in serious difficulty, when his life is trembling in the balance, or when he is in acute agony?" Why then, O Sceptics, do you deny the existence of God? You yourself admit His existence when you are in trouble On account of perverted intellect and worldly intoxication you have turned out as an atheist Is this not a great folly? Think seriously Give up arguing Remember Him and attain Immortality and eternal peace right now

In Garuda Purana and Atma Purana it is described that the pangs of death are tantamount to the pain caused by the stings of 72,000 scorpions. This is only mentioned to induce fear (Bhayanaka Sabda) in the hearers and readers and force them to work for Moksha. In spiritualism there is the unanimous report from enlightened spirits that there is not even a bit of pain during death They clearly describe their experiences at death and state that they are relieved of a great burden of this physical body and that they enjoy perfect composure at the time of separation from the physical body Maya induces vain fear in the on -lookers by inducing convulsive twitchings of the body That is her nature and habit Don't be afraid of death pangs You are immortal (Amara)

Strive ceaselessly to live in God through Japa, Kirtan, service of the poor and meditation Then only will you be able to conquer Time or Death

When the God of Death comes to take your life, he will not accept your excuses "I had no time to worship God in my life"

Knowledge of Brahman or Brahma Jnana alone can free us from the clutches of ignorance and death This knowledge should come to us as a direct realisation through meditation Mere scholarship or intelligence or study of religious books cannot help us to attain the *summum bonum* It is a matter of direct experience and not of argument or reasoning

Habitual study of abstract problems will result in another earthly life, in a well-developed power for abstract thinking, while flippant, hasty thinking, flying from one object to another, will bequeath a restless ill-regulated mind to the birth following this world

Self-realisation will remove Avidya or ignorance, the root-cause of human sufferings, and produce in you the knowledge of oneness of the Self, which is the means for eradicating grief, delusion, the dire malady of birth and death the concomitants of Samsara or world's process

The Sun of pure consciousness is shining in the chambers of your heart This spiritual Sun of suns is self-luminous It is the Self of all beings, that transcends speech and mind If you realise this Self, you will no more return to this Mrityuloka, the world of death

Birth and death are two illusory scenes in the drama of this world, created by the jugglery of Maya In truth, nobody comes and nobody goes. Atma alone exists for ever Destroy fear and Moha through enquiry and rest in peace.

I know that mighty Purusha who, resplendent like the Sun, transcends darkness (ignorance) By knowing Him alone, one conquers Death There is no other way to salvation" (Yajur Veda XXXI—181)

Every effort in the direction of Yoga never goes in vain You will realise thereby the fruit of even a little Yogic practice If you have succeeded in the practice of the three limbs of Yoga in this birth viz, Yama, Niyama and Asana, you will begin your practice in the next birth from the fourth limb, viz., Pranayama A Vedantin who has acquired two means, viz, Viveka and Vairagya in this birth, will start his practice in the next birth from the sixfold virtues, viz, Sama, Dama, etc Therefore, you should not be discouraged a bit even, if you fail to attain the Kaivalya or independence or final Asamprajnata Samadhi in this birth Even a little practice for a short period will give you more strength, more peace, more joy and more knowledge

You cannot die, because you were never born You are immortal Atman Birth and death are two false scenes in the unreal drama of Maya They concern the physical sheath only, a false product formed by the combination of the five elements The ideas of birth and death are mere superstition

This physical body which is made up of clay or earth is a toy for the Lord for His Lila or sporting He is the wire-puller or Sutradhar He keeps His toy running as long as He likes Eventually He breaks the toy and throws the pieces away The game of two ceases There is only oneness The individual soul merges in the Supreme Soul

The knowledge of the Self destroys all fear of death People are unnecessarily alarmed of death Death is like sleep Birth is like waking up from sleep in the morning. Just as you put on new clothes, so also you put on a new body after death Death is a natural incident in its course It is necessary for your evolution When the physical body becomes unfit for further activities and use, Lord Rudra takes it away and supplies a new body There is no pain at the time of death Ignorant people have created much horror and terror regarding death

There is only one Reality—Brahman This world and body are superimposed on Brahman, just as snake is superimposed on the rope As long as the rope is not known and the idea of snake persists, you are not free from fear. Similarly this world is a solid reality to you until Brahman is realised When you see the rope with a light, the illusion of snake vanishes and the fear disappears Even so, when you realise Brahman, this world vanishes and you are freed from the fear of births and deaths

You dream sometimes that you are dead and that your relatives are weeping Even in that supposed death-state, you see and hear them weeping This clearly indicates that even after apparent death, life really persists You exist even after the physical sheath is thrown out That existence is Atman or the big 'I'

If you realise this immortal soul which is hidden in your heart, if the three knots viz, Avidya (ignorance), Kama (desire) and Karma (action) are rent asunder, if the chain of ignorance viz, ignorance, non-discrimination, egoism, likes and dislikes Karma, body, is broken, you will be freed from the round of births and deaths, and you will enter the city of deathlessness

Seek the Immortal

O Man! what have you to do with wealth, bungalows and gardens? What have you to do with friends and relatives? What have you to do with wife and children? What have you to do with power, name, fame, position and prestige? You will surely die Everything is uncertain here but death is certain Seek the immortal Atman or the Imperishable Self which is hidden in the chambers of your heart.

Spiritual wealth is real inexhaustible wealth Divine knowledge is real knowledge. Find out the way to conquer Death Realise the Eternal Atman and attain freedom and perfection, eternity and immortality

The happy-go-lucky worldly man does not care for religion and higher transcendental matters He does not worry about God, doctrine of reincarnation, Immortal Soul, Yoga Sadhana, the four means He knows two things well, viz, to fill his pocket and to fill his belly He eats, drinks jokes, sleeps, procreates and dresses himself in different costumes

Some cross the seas to get University degrees Some practise alchemy to turn copper into gold Some practise Pranayama to live for hundred years Some do banking and business to amass immense wealth If you reflect deeply for a while you will find out these people do two things only viz., eating sumptuously and sleeping Nothing more than this

But their eyes are opened a bit when their dearest relative dies, when they get an incurable disease, when they lose their wealth They get a temporary disgust for worldly life They ask "What is life? What is death? What is there on the other side of death? Is there any life beyond? Where shall we go after death?" The dispassion soon vanishes as they have no discrimination

Man tries to find happiness in sensual objects Too much sensual indulgence wears out the senses and brings disgust, sickness, and diseases of all kinds The more sexual pleasures he enjoys, the greater the passion becomes. He learns bitter lessons He learns that his happiness does not lie in satisfying the desire of the body and the senses

At last he seeks to find happiness in his own Atman within

If you oppress a man you will suffer oppression in another life and reap the fruit of the seed you have sown in this life If you injure the eye of a man your eye will be injured in another life If you break the leg of a man your leg will be broken in another life If you feed the poor, you will have plenty of food in another life If you build rest-houses you will have many houses in another life Action and reaction are equal and opposite Such is the law of Karma Such is the law of birth and death Such is the circle through which you must pass on your way.

Many people are rich but they do not enjoy their life properly. They have plenty of money. They have many bungalows and yet they are unhappy Their life is very miserable. They suffer from several chronic diseases Their sons are vagabonds They are miserly. They are disliked by their friends and relatives How do you account for this? They craved for money in their previous births and so they had it in this life but did not use it well They were selfish and cruel in their past life They had no character in their previous birth So they suffer in this birth

Do good actions Entertain sublime, divine thoughts and build your character. Have one, pure, holy desire. the desire for liberation from the wheel of birth and death

Your character is built by your thoughts As you think, so shall you become. If you think nobly you will be born with a noble character If you think badly you will be born with a bad character. This is the immutable law of nature.

Desire determines which sort of objects you will have in your next life. If you desire wealth very much you will get it in your next life. If you desire power very much you will get it in your next life. But money and power cannot give you eternal bliss and immortality. You must be very careful in your choice. Entertain one strong desire, the desire for Moksha or the final emancipation. Shun worldly desires ruthlessly. You will soon be freed from the round of births and deaths.

CHAPTER TEN

STORIES

Story of a Worm

Yudhishthira said

1 "Wishing to die and wishing to live many persons surrender their lives in the great sacrifice (of battle) Tell me, O grandfather, what is the end that these attain to?

2—3 "To give up life in battle is fraught with sorrow for men O you of great wisdom, you know that to give up life is difficult for men whether they are rich or poor, or are in happiness or misery In my opinion, you are gifted with omniscience Do tell me the reason of this"

Bhishma said

4 "In prosperity or adversity, in weal or woe, living creatures, O King! coming into this world, live according to a particular method

5 "Listen to me as I explain the reason to you. The question you have put to me is, indeed, excellent, O Yudhishthira!

6 "Regarding it, O King! I shall explain to you the old dialogue that took place between the Dwaipayana Rishi and a crawling worm.

7 "Formerly when the learned Brahmana, viz, the Krishna Dwaipayana, having identified himself with Brahma, roamed over the world, he saw on a road over which cars used to pass, a worm moving quickly

8 "The Rishi knew the course of every creature and the language of every animal Gifted with omniscience, he addressed the worm in these words

9 "O worm, you appear to be greatly alarmed. and to be in great haste Tell me, where do you run. and whence have you been afraid?"

The worm said:

10 "I am stricken with fear on hearing the rattle of that large cart O you! of great intelligence, it makes a fearful roar It is almost come.

11 "The sound is heard Will it not kill me? I am flying away from this I hear the sound of the bulls

12 "They are breathing hard under the whip of the driver, as they are carrying the heavy load I hear also the various sounds made by the men who are driving the bulls

13. "Creatures like us born as worms, cannot bear such sounds It is, therefore, that I am flying from this situation of great fright.

14 "Death is considered by all creatures as painful. Life is an acquisition difficult to make Hence I fly away in fear, I do not wish to pass from a state of weal to one of woe."

Bhishma said

15 "Thus addressed, Dwaipayana Vyasa said: 'O worm, whence can be your happiness? You belong

to the intermediate order of being I think, death would be of happiness to you

16 "Sound, touch taste, scent, and various kinds of excellent enjoyments are unknown to you. O worm! I think death will prove a benefit to you'"

The worm said

17 'A living creature however circumstanced it may be, becomes attached to it Even in this order of being I am happy, I think, O you of great wisdom! It is for this that I wish to live

18 "In this condition every object of enjoyment exists for me according to the necessity of my body Human beings and those creatures which originate from immobile objects have different enjoyments

19 "In my former life I was a human being, O powerful one I was a wealthy Shudra I was not devoted to the Brahmanas I was cruel, vile in conduct, and an usurer

20 'I was harsh in speech I considered cunning as wisdom I hated all creatures Taking advantage of pretexts in agreements made between myself and others, I used always to take away what belonged to others

21 "Without feeding servants and guests who came to my home, I used to fill, when hungry, my own stomach, proud, greedy of good food, cruel as I was

22 "Covetous as I was of riches, I never dedicated with faith and respect any food to the celestials and the departed Manes, although duty enjoined me to dedicate food to them.

23 "Those men who moved by fear came to me for seeking my help, I sent them adrift without giving any protection I did not extend my help to those who came to me with prayer for removing their fear.

24 "I used to feel unreasonable envy at seeing other peoples' riches, and corn, and wives held dear by them and articles of drink, and good palaces

25. "Seeing the happiness of others, I was filled with envy and I always wished them poverty. Acting thus which promised to crown my own wishes with fruition, I sought to destroy the virtue, riches and pleasures of other people.

26 "In that past life of mine, I committed various deeds moved by cruelty and such other passions. Recollecting those deeds, I am filled with repentance and grief, as one is filled with grief at the loss of his dear son.

27 'On account of those deeds of mine, I do not know what the fruits of good deeds are I, however, adored my old mother and on one occasion adored a Brahmana

28 "Gifted with birth and accomplishments, that Brahmana, while travelling, came to my house once as a guest I received him with respectful hospitality On account of the merit of that deed my memory has not forsaken me

29 "I think that on account of that deed I shall once more succeed in regaining happiness Having asceticism for wealth, you know everything Tell me please what is for my behalf.'

(Anushasanika Parva—Maha Bharata)

Story of Nachiketas

I think you all remember the story of Nachiketas, which is narrated in the Kathopanishad Gautama, the father of Nachiketas, was performing a sacrifice Nachiketas asked his father "To whom will you give me?" The father replied. "To Death I will give you"

Nachiketas went to the house of Yama, the Lord of Death He stood there for three days and nights without receiving any hospitality, as Yama had gone out and as there was none to receive him The Lord of Death returned and found Nachiketas waiting in obedience to his father's promise to give him to Death

Yama said to Nachiketas "O Brahmin! as thou, a venerable guest, hast dwelt in my house three nights without eating, choose now three boons in return" Then Nachiketas first asked that his father might again be pleased with him. Yama said. "Your father will recognise you as before He will sleep peacefully at night and when he sees you released from me, he will lose his anger."

The second boon was that of the heavenly fire and Yama said that that fire will be known to him and called by his name As for the third boon, the boy asked for the secret of Death. "There is that doubt, when a man is dead—some say he is and some say he is not—this! I should like to know. Tell me, O Lord of Death, thy secret Can man escape from thy clutch?"

Yama said· "Do not ask that On this point even the gods of olden times had doubt. Verily, it is not easy to understand it Subtle is its nature O! Nachiketas, choose another boon Do not press me on this point I will give you sons, grandsons, gold, horses, dominions, wealth, long life, fair damsels to attend on you, chariots etc "

Nachiketas said "These things are ephemeral They wear out the vigour of all the senses Even the longest life is short It is nothing when compared to Eternity Keep thou thy chariots, the damsels the dance and music No one can be made happy by wealth Give me the one boon, the only boon I seek—How may man escape thy mouth?'

Lord Yama found out that the boy was a qualified student for the attainment of Jnana or wisdom of the Soul He told him how man might escape from the hands of Death. He said "O Nachiketas ! Just listen to me with rapt attention I shall tell you the way to attain Immortality Man is bound by desires The desires are born of the senses These bind him to the wheel of birth and death He must destroy the desires and subjugate the mind and the senses This is the first step to be taken The body is like a chariot, the senses are the horses, the mind is the reins and the intellect is the driver The Atman or the Self is the Lord of the chariot The sensual objects are the roads The horses gallop after the objects of senses and carry the chariot with them They must be guided along the right path He who has no discrimination and whose mind is always uncontrolled, his senses (horses) are not controlled like the turbulent horses of a driver He does not reach the goal, but enters into the round of births and deaths But, he, who has understanding and whose mind is always controlled, his senses are under control like the good trained horses of a driver He reaches that goal whence he is not born again He reaches the end of his journey, that highest place of Vishnu

"Meditate on the One, the Eternal, the Atman, which dwells in the cavity of the heart Fix your mind on the Supreme Self When all the desires of the senses are destroyed, when the three knots of ignorance are broken, then you will attain Immortality or Self-realisation or Brahma Jnana Thus you may conquer Death O Nachiketas! This is the secret of Death

'This Atman cannot be found by the sensual or the weak It cannot be attained by arguments or discourse or study The Self reveals Himself to him alone whom He chooses The choice of the Self is determined by the purity and unselfishness of the life of the aspirant

'Arise! Awake! Having reached the great Teachers, learn and realise that wonderful Atman Like the sharp edge of a razor is that path, difficult to cross and hard to tread—thus the wise say."

Nachiketas then having acquired this knowledge imparted by Yama and also the whole teaching about Yoga, having become free from passion, all impurities and death, attained Brahman or the Immortal Soul Thus it will be with others also who thus know the nature of the Atman or the Immortal Soul

Story of Markandeya

Markandeya was a great devotee of Lord Siva. His father Mrikandu performed rigorous austerities to get a son Lord Siva appeared before him and said: "O Rishi! Do you want a good son who will die in his sixteenth year or a bad and foolish son who will live for a long time" Mrikandu replied, "O my venerable Lord! Let me have a good son"

The boy came to know about his fate and began to worship Lord Siva whole-heartedly with intense faith and devotion The boy entered into deep meditation and Samadhi on the day decreed as the day of his death Hence Yama himself went to take his life The boy prayed to Lord Siva for protection and embraced the Linga Then Yama threw his noose round the Linga and the boy Lord Siva came out of the Linga immediately and killed Yama to protect the boy Lord Siva was called Mrityunjaya and Kalakala from that day

Then the Devas approached Lord Siva and said "O Adorable Lord! Salutations unto Thee Pardon Yama for his mistake, O Ocean of Mercy, bring him back to his life" Then Lord Siva brought Yama back to life at the request of the gods He also conferred a boon on the boy Markandeya, that he should live for ever as a boy of sixteen years of age He is a Chiranjivi In South India, even now men and women bless a boy when he does prostration to them. "Live as Chiranjivi Markandeya"

Through Tapas and meditation you can conquer death, you can achieve anything in the three worlds

CHAPTER ELEVEN

LETTERS

Where is my Husband's Soul?

Sri Swami Sivananda,
Ananda Kutir, Rishikesh.

Most Revered Swamiji'

Many thanks for your kind letter which was a great consolation to me in my sorrow.

I would like to know very much where my husband's soul is at present and what happens to the soul from the time it leaves the body till it is reborn again I tried to follow the article in the Divine Life Magazine, on the "Soul's Journey after Death", but could not understand some parts especially from the 2nd para on page 261

I feel, I will be able to understand your explanation more clearly than others So, I shall be obliged if you could explain to me what happens to the soul after death and what merits we could do for the peace of the departed soul and whether he could see or hear us, mortals Is there any truth in what the spiritualists say that we could commune with the dead through a thing called "medium" and is it really the dead person who answers?

Your humble disciple.

Ananda Kutir,
12th Feb., '45

Blessed Divinity!

Salutations and Adorations.

Thy kind line. Do not allow yourself to be fascinated by spiritualism, mediumship, crystal gazing, etc. They will lead you astray. Communication with the dead and talking with the dead are all fads which have no connection with real spirituality. Purpose of life is different. The goal is to realise the essential imperishability of your Self. This alone will confer perfect bliss and peace.

The spirit is neither born nor does it die. Like a person passing from one room to another the soul passes from one plane of existence to another. In the period between death and rebirth the individual works out certain of his Karmas in subtler spheres. The description of the journey and return of the soul in the article mentioned by your good self is meant to explain the idea how the spirit passes gradually from grosser to subtler states. The mention of ether, air, smoke, mist, cloud, rain is all made to convey the sense of successive degrees of subtlety. At the appointed time it takes up a new body again.

The best means of ensuring peace for the departed is to do Kirtan, increase your Japa, relieve other peoples' distress, by selfless service and charity and earnest prayer.

Do not try to commune with the departed soul of your husband. Communion with the departed soul will stand in the way of its onward march to higher, blissful regions and make it earth-bound. Do not try to drag him down It will disturb his peace. The spirit guide which controls the medium is ignorant and deceitful It utters falsehood

Thy own Self,
Sivananda

Where is Heaven?

5th August, 1943

Respected Sir,

In the August Number of the "Divine Life" there is an article titled "Ritu Dharma", the last part of which I find a bit confusing It gives

"Jiva moves to heaven after physical body is cast off, stays there till the fruits of Karma are exhausted, comes down to the earth through the rains and gets mixed with the grains, enters the semen of the man and the womb with the semen Further on soul enters the foetus in the seventh month."

I shall be much obliged if I am enlightened on the following points in this connection

1 Where is the heaven where the soul goes and how does it reach there Evidently it needs the support of raindrops to come down and therefore it must need something to go up

2 Raindrops can be available only from the cloud area Apparently heaven does not coincide with the clouds If so, how does Jiva come to the clouds from heaven

3 I understand, our Samsar is not only Karmasthan but also Bhogasthan If so, how is it that Jiva is said to exhaust the fruits of his Karmas in the

heaven and return to earth after exhausting them there.

4 Jiva is said to enter the womb with the semen of man and then the soul is described to enter the foetus in the 7th month. How are the two facts to be reconciled? Is Jiva different from soul? If so, what is the difference, if not, how do these two statements arise?

Yours faithfully,
KBR

Rev Immortal Self,

Salutations and adorations Thy kind letter of the 5th

The Jiva can travel in space. It need not necessarily have any physical support like raindrops, earth etc It finds entrance into this physical world through raindrops, that is all There are seven planes which are interpenetrating one subtler than the other Heaven is one of them.

Our physical world is meant for evolution through the performance of good Karmas and spiritual Sadhana At the same time, the individual soul meets with pleasure or pain which is the result of his good or bad Karma Bhoga is very negligible when compared to suffering . Suffering alone makes a man really wise and introspective In Svarga there is only Bhoga and no pain

Till the seventh month the Jiva remains in an unmanifested state "The soul enters the foetus in the seventh month"—this does not mean that it newly enters It only means that it begins to manifest in the seventh month when the formation of the physical body completes

May you prosper gloriously in the spiritual path! May God bless you With kind regards Prem and OM

Thy Own Self
SIVANANDA

What About my Child?

Sri Guru Charana Kamalebhyo Namah

Received your kind letter which has given me great peace

Revered Swamiji! my following points remain unanswered and I request you to throw light

1 Gita XIV 14-15 describes about the next birth of those meeting death when Sattva, Rajas and Tamas are predominant In the present state the child was senseless

Gita XIII-6 states that the last thoughts determine the next birth Can a child of 5 years be expected to possess any thinking-power in senseless state So what birth is he likely to attain?

2 Can he or his soul be benefited through Japa and charity done on his behalf? I feel he has left this world without doing any Sadhana

3 I believe the prayers have their effects, but there is a room for doubt on the ground that the man reaps the fruits according to his action. The Divine law is immutable

4 Is the span of life fixed before birth?

Your humble etc.

A:—The boy has worked out some very powerful, bad Karmas of the last birth by meeting death at his 5th year Now he is free from that evil Karma He will get a good birth in which he will be in a position to do more Sadhana

The essence of a man's thinking in his whole life constitutes his last thought or Bhav If a man is senseless, the last thought or Bhav which he has just before entering the unconscious state will determine his next birth

Prayers have very beneficial results Just as you can help your son in Germany with money and advice, you can help him in this and in the other world by your prayers Good and sublime thoughts and prayers have a very soothing effect and they will help to mould one's own nature and those of others around him

The span of life is predestined None can overstep the limits of Kala (time) Time sweeps away everything in the world from the smallest ant to that of Brahma

Prasnottari

Q·—How long will the soul remain in heaven?

A —It can remain for fifty years or five hundred years It depends upon the nature and degree of meritorious actions done by the man on earth plane

Q —Is the year in heaven same as in earth plane?

A —No Ten years of the earth plane is equal to ten days for the Devas in the heaven.

Q —What takes place just before death?

A —The soul contracts and withdraws all the senses The physical senses become dimmer just as the flame in a lamp becomes dimmer and dimmer when the oil gets exhausted.

Q —How does it pass out of the body?

A —The subtle body or Sukshma Sarira passes out of the physical body like a mist

Q —Through which opening does the soul leave the body?

A —So long as Prana pulls up and Apana pulls down the life-forces, there is continuity of life But the moment either of these becomes weaker, there is an exit of the life-force If the Apana gives way then Jiva will pass out of the body through either the head or the nose or the ear or the mouth If the Prana gives way then it will pass out of the body through the anus

Q —Will spiritualism help one to go beyond birth and death?

A —Certainly not Knowledge of the Imperishable Soul or Brahma Jnana alone can destroy the cycle of births and deaths and confer on you immortality and eternal bliss

Q —Can a departed soul take birth immediately?

A —It can But such instances are rare. If the soul has an intense desire to be reborn, it will take its birth immediately The soul has to reap its fruits of Karmas in heaven or hell. If it takes rebirth immediately it can remember many of the events of its previous life

Q.—How long should the soul wait for getting a body?

A.—Nothing definite can be said on this point Great souls will have to wait for a long time

Q.—Can the departed spirit take the power of materialisation?

A.—Only advanced spirits who are endowed with psychic power are able to materialise They take human form, sit in the chair in the seance and shake hands with those who sit in the seance They talk also The touch is as tangible and warm as that of a living human body. In a short time the hand of the spirit melts away Photographs of the spirits also have been taken

Q.—What is astral body?

A.—Astral body is the subtle body which is within this physical body like the bladder of a football It is exact counterpart of the physical body. It is made up of five organs of actions, five organs of knowledge, five Pranas, viz., mind intellect, Chitta or subconscious mind and Ahamkar or egoism Some call it as "double" It is this astral body that comes out of the physical body after death and moves to heaven Death of this astral body through the knowledge of the Eternal frees one from the cycle of births and deaths

Q.—What is the difference between Metempsychosis and reincarnation?

A.—Metempsychosis is transmigration of a human soul into an animal form Reincarnation is the rebirth of the same ego in successive human bodies

Q·—Why do we not remember our past lives?

A —Such remembrance under our existing limitations would considerably complicate our present life Therefore, the wise and beneficent Lord has so ordered our mental evolution that we cannot recall our past lives until such time as it is good and helpful for us to remember Such instances may well form a cycle which is all clear to us when we have come to the end of it, when we shall see a whole rosary of lives threaded upon the one personality

Q —It has been said against reincarnation that there are more people in comparison with the past world population?

A.—It is not necessary that the same persons are reborn, and none else In the process of evolution into the human life many from lower births also come up to the human level All these are controlled by superhuman powers or by the Divinity God or Ishvar Himself. Further rebirth need not necessarily be on this earth plane alone It can take place anywhere in the Universe

Q —What account do you give for the origin of a person's existence?

A.—Existence is the nature of a person. He is always existing No proof is needed His existence is endless and beginningless Hence no origin can be traced of one's existence

Q:—Some men and women find their bodies awkward. Why?

A:—It is the past Karma of an individual that is responsible for the awkwardness or otherwise of one's appearance

Q.—With reincarnation is there turn about sexes?

A —Sex can change in rebirth, but need not always

Q —Do you think that Mahatma Gandhi might escape the necessity of a rebirth?

A —It is a Divine Secret The status of great men, and great souls, depends on the Divine dispensation

Q —How long does it take for souls to be reborn?

A —This is also decided by the Lord It is not for man to guess or know such truths It is beyond his realm

Q —Regarding reincarnation, Jesus Christ forgives our sins, so how can you explain that we come back to make amends

A.—According to Hindu belief all Karmas have to be worked out Even if sins are forgiven one has to work his way for salvation by practising Yoga and uniting himself with God.

Q —How could we incarnate if women would not bear children any more?

A —Such a contingency would never arise You need not be afraid of that condition

APPENDICES

APPENDIX I

Sojourn in Heaven

When the virtuous people die, they move towards, and live in Heaven. The period of their sojourn in Heaven may extend from eighty to two-hundred-and-forty years, it is popularly believed. They are, after the termination of their period of stay in Heaven, again reborn on earth

After death, the virtuous people enjoy the pleasures of Heaven as a reward of their merits, their virtuous deeds their services and their sacrifices When their merits are exhausted they return to earth

Lord Krishna says in the Bhagavadgita *Te tam bhuktva svargalokam visalam, ksheene punye martyalokam visanti evam trayeedharmamanuprapanna gatagatam kamakama labhante.* They, having enjoyed the spacious heaven world, their holiness withered, come back to this world of death Following the virtues enjoyed by the scriptures, desiring desires, they obtain the transitory

But, when a virtuous person comes back from Heaven, to the physical world, he takes birth in noble and virtuous families This is the advantage of virtuous deeds. There is double retribution or reward for man's virtuous actions. He gets after his sojourn in Heaven, and return to the earth, a good birth with good surroundings, environments and opportunities for his good actions and inner evolution

Jnani After Death

For a Jnani who has realised the identity of his inner Being with the Infinite Brahman, there is no rebirth, no migration, not even liberation for he is already liberated He has firmly established in an experience of the absolute Existence, Knowledge, Bliss, the Satchidananda Atman.

The continued existence of the world and of his own body appears to the Jnani, only as an illusion, the appearance of which he cannot remove, but which cannot further deceive him, till the time when, after the decease of the body, he wanders not forth, but remains where he is and what he is and eternally was, the first Principle of all beings and things, the original, eternal, pure, free Brahman

While living and even when the body falls dead, the Jnani rests in his own essential Nature, his own Svaroopa that is all-full, all-pure, timeless Consciousness and Bliss The following assertions made by a Jnani constitute his own deepest convictions and experience.

I am Infinite, imperishable, self-luminous, self-existent. I am beginningless endless, decayless, birthless, deathless Never was I born I am ever free, perfect, independent; I alone am, I pervade the entire universe; I am all-permeating and inter-penetrating, I am supreme Peace and Freedom Absolute.

A Jnani lives for ever, he has attained life everlasting Cravings torture him not, sins stain him not; birth and death touch him not, he is free from all cravings and longings, he ever rests in his own Satchidananda-swaroopa He sees the one Infinite Self in all, and all in the Infinite Self which is his being, he remains for ever as the Infinite Self of Consciousness and Delight

Rebirth and Evolution of Man

The question of rebirth, of life after death, has remained an enigma through ages. Human knowledge is hardly capable of answering all the problems that life foreshadows, and as Gautama Buddha would say, "In this world of forms and illusions created by our senses according to our illusions, a man either is or is not, either lives or dies, but in the true and formless world this is not so, for all is otherwise than according to our knowledge, and if you ask, does a man live beyond death, I answer No, not in any sense comprehensible to the mind of man which itself dies at death, and if you ask, does a man altogether die at death, I answer No, for what dies is what belongs to this world of form and illusion"

Yet, human mind would not allow itself to be puzzled by a mystic answer without a definite conclusion, and the age of implicit belief in what the wise had said once upon a time is long past Today we have a perpetual demand for concrete evidence *en masse*, not of solitary prodigies But if such be the attitude on a profound mystery like the soul's transmigration, the obvious answer has to be , "Better wait until you die, and then you can conclusively know."

There arises therefore the necessity of a cool, rational, dispassionate and impersonal consideration

The doctrine of cause and effect and the consequent inevitability of reincarnation has been the very bedrock of the Hindu philosophy But ignore we cannot, the obvious fact that out of 2000 millions of the earth's population over 800 millions have no religious tradition to believe in rebirth, while nearly 540 millions are quite agnostic about its possibility

Naturally, then it will be a sheer rodomontade of the Hindus thought that they were the wisest of men, as though the rest were a massive bunch of ignorant persons, to whom ignorance was bliss Then the question will arise if one is to believe that his present life is resultant of the actions done in his previous birth, what was it that caused that previous birth? Well, another previous birth. But what was the cause of that birth, again?

Now, to answer this, we have to fall back upon the law of evolution and say that in the long, distant past we had been once animals and from that strata of life we become human beings But the question would again arise that in order to justify the theory of cause and effect there must have been some cause as well to be born as human beings, and since animals have no intellect to judge between virtue and vice, how could we be held responsible for our birth into the family of Man? Does not matter, let us tentatively accept this illogical hypothesis to be true, and lead ourselves back into the family of worms and then into the vegetable and the mineral kingdoms, and finally arrive at the conclusion that God must have been the original cause responsible But, believing in the theory of cause and effect, how indeed, for all the world of reason, could God be so unjust and undeniably become the original cause for all the suffering, conflict and unhappiness that we must undergo, born as we are as human beings?

There is no answer for the original cause. The best course is Be good and do good, believe in a good conscience and respect the worthiness of the individual and the ethics of life, leaving the rest to God. There are many things beyond the orbit of the human mind, and knowledge of the Self, however imposing the term might be, is the only answer to them Nevertheless the concept of rebirth cannot be so easily brushed aside, since there are substantial logical inferences, which yield a strong influence on reason to sustain faith

In the early phases of the Vedic literature there is practically no reference to rebirth and no stigma of sins, no dread of the hell-fire and no heavenly lure for the mortals But with the beginning of the Aranyaka period as the Vedic mind progressed from a polytheistic concept of the elemental godhead towards a monistic ideal of the one, absolute Reality, the doctrine of cause and effect and the transmigration of soul was evolved as a logical necessity in order to safeguard an unsullied existence of God in human thought

Now, it is quite well-known that three of the leading religions of the world, though much younger to Hinduism in origin, found it necessary to present a dreadful prospect of an eternal devilment in the hell so that men might desist from flying at each other's throat and respect social harmony, the value of culture and the usefulness of peace A colourful lure of a joyous immortality in the heaven was offered at the same time, directed only to serve the same purpose But here was at once discredited the principle of evolution and man was either abruptly condemned to hell without a slight after-chance of redemption, or he was overgraciously suspended in the heaven for eternity, with an individualised existence Nor was there any answer as to why one man should be flourishing and happy in spite of being wicked and another should be drudging on a life of want, full of wretchedness, in spite of being virtuous

The Indian sages, on the contrary offered a better solution and made reincarnation responsible for the evolution of man who alone was the master of his destiny They frankly admitted their incapability of answering why the world should have been created at all, and from that basis asserted that God was not responsible for good and evil, happiness and suffering, but it was man who was responsible for the decree of his fate, capable at the same time of its betterment through his own self-effort So, God could not be accused for all the baffling inequalities and injustices of life, and His position in human thought was kept unscathed The theory of reincarnation is, therefore, a far more convincing doctrine than any belief that justifies an arbitrary irredemption after death

Furthermore, we have many examples as to how a child easily becomes an adept artist or a gifted musician with very little of training, whereas in some aristocratic families we find that in spite of tremendous efforts of highly qualified teachers and arduous toil on the part of the youngster himself, he is able to make very little progress in learning There are also the examples of child prodigies with no background of training Take another case There are two children born of the same parents and brought up under the same environments one of them turns out to be a brilliant scholar with fine manners, and the other becomes a dull-headed ragamuffin for no apparent reason at all The theory of rebirth alone might answer for the difference

Rebirth is life's sustaining force, even from the worldly point of view So many dreams and so many eagerly-sought-after ambitions remain unfulfilled; youth gradually decays into old age and infirmity, and the amber of elusive hope gets dimmer and weaker, but its flame is kept up flickering by a remote expectation that perhaps in another birth those dreams might be fulfilled So, even from this point of view, rebirth is indeed a gentle consolation and a solace to life

There is another school of thought which believes that the sledge-hammer of death puts a final end to life, the body and the soul having passed out into the five elements in ultimate oblivion. This convenient belief is very appealing to some intellectual sophists But if such be the case, then what is to account for the apparitions and the undeniable experiences at a seance? Hence, life after death cannot be ruled out Now, let us take into consideration as to what should be the attitude of a spiritual aspirant

Man has a tremendous potentiality within himself He is not the slave of fate Once Buddha asked

Sariputta, one of his most brilliant disciples, to whom the world owes an immense debt for the establishment of Buddhism, "Well, monk, does not life burden you and don't you like to be released by death? Or, does living fascinate you, because there is a noble mission to fulfil?" Sariputta replied, "Venerable Teacher, I desire not life. I desire not death. I wait until my hour shall come, like a servant that waits for his wage."

Even so should be the attitude of an aspirant. He has nothing to fulfil of his own, since his life is a fulfilment of the will of God. Even the desire to be born again in order to foster a worthy spiritual mission should find no place in him. For, does not God know better as to whom to send as His messenger to this world? And is it not man's highest ideal to rejoice in the dissolution of his body and the mind and his individuality in the great cosmic oneness of the Absolute, and thus once for all cease to be an individualised consciousness either astrally existent or physically imprisoned.

Most assuredly does every aspirant reserve the right to disclaim rebirth for himself, because liberation is his birthright and he is the master of his destiny. No obsession is ever good, be it spiritual or temporal. It is better to cleanse the mind of any unhealthy fear-complex than be harrowed by an obsession at the time of death. Having known the evanescent nature of the material values of life, one has to deny the prospect of being crucified again inside his prison-house of flesh and blood, and claim one's legitimate due with all the vigour and intensity of will and thought that he can command.

Thought decides action and action decides destiny There is a vast reservoir of power within every individual and one can surely pulverise any possibility of a future life by the sheer force of his will, together with the inevitable grace of God, and so modelling his present life as to leave no trace of earthly ambition and no tell-tale of an unwipable mark of stigmatic actions Did not Dattatreya, the sage of unparalleled wisdom and renunciation say, "For the initiated there is no rebirth?"

Retrogression into Animal Births

Hindu scriptures say that a man may become a Deva or a beast or a bird or vegetable or stone according to his merit or demerit The Upanishads also corroborate this statement Kapila also agrees on this point.

But Buddhism and some Western philosophers teach "There is no more retrogression for a man when once he takes a human birth. There is no necessity for him to be born as an animal for the sake of demerit He can be punished in a variety of ways in the human birth itself"

When a man takes the form of a Deva, all human Samskaras, habits and tendencies will remain dormant When a man takes the form of a dog, the animal-tendencies, habits and Samskaras only will manifest Human tendencies will remain suppressed. Some dogs get royal treatment in the palaces of kings and aristocratic people They move in cars, eat good food and sleep in cushions These are all degenerated human beings

Linga-Sarira Survives Death of Physical Body

After death this physical body composed of five elements is cast off like a slough or the coil of a snake The inner astral body or Linga-Sarira which consists of nineteen Tattvas, viz, five Karma Indriyas five Jnana Indriyas, five Pranas, mind, Buddhi, Chitta and Ahamkara goes to heaven, comes back to the physical plane puts on another physical body and reincarnates

It is this Linga-Sarira or astral body that contains the impressions of all past Karmas This body remains till one gets knowledge and realisation of the Self, and consequent emancipation Then, it disintegrates and the components get involved in the ocean of Tanmatras or Avyaktam

Nature of the Next Birth

The last powerful thought that occupies the mind of a man in his dying moment determines the nature of his next birth If the thought of tea comes to your mind at the moment of death, you may become a manager of a tea-estate in the next birth, if you have done virtuous actions or you may be born as a coolie in a tea-estate if you had not done any meritorious action

A drunkard will have thoughts of liquor when he is dying A licentious man will think of woman only when he is about to expire I saw a dying man who had the habit of using snuff When he was in an unconscious state he used to move his fingers towards the nose very often and do imaginary snuffing Obviously he had thought of snuff A medical officer of a hospital, who was given over to using abusive words, used all sorts of abusive obscene terms when he was in a dying condition King Jada Bharata, as I have already stated elsewhere, took great care of a deer out of compassion He gradually developed attachment The one thought of deer alone occupied his mind when he was in the dying state So, he had to take the birth of a deer

In every Hindu home the Names of God such as Hari, Om, Ram, Narayana, are blown into the ears of the dying man The principle is that the dying man may remember the name and form of God and thereby reach the blissful abode If a man leads a virtuous life for many years and if he does japa and meditation on God for a long time, then alone through the force of habit he may remember God and His Name at the moment of death

Vedantic View of Heaven and Hell

According to Vedanta, heaven and hell are purely mental creations The Joys of Heaven are spoken of only to persuade the virtuous to greater deeds of virtue goodness, love and service The torments of hell are presented only to dissuade the wicked people from their wicked, unrighteous, evil harmful deeds

By purity goodness love, service, the human mind forms around itself, its own Heaven, by impurity error, evil ignorance the human mind creates for itself suffering and sorrow that go by the name of hell It is true as poet Milton sang, Mind is its own place, and can in itself make a heaven or a hell

Man is, in his true and essential inner spiritual Nature, eternal, unborn, infinite, of the Nature of

Light, Joy, Peace. It is Ignorance that is the root-cause of his suffering, limitations, individuality, error, birth and death. Self-realisation, the experience of the Infinite Self within himself, releases man into the Kingdom of Infinite Peace, Freedom and Bliss.

That there is an independent plane of existence called hell, subsisting in its own right, is fully supported by the Pauranic literature. Suppose there is a wicked and inveterate drunkard given over to insensibility of every type and vice. After death he is led by the Messengers of Death to that plane of existence called Hell, and left to suffer the torments of a Tantalus, the tortures of moving in scorching deserts where his agonising thirst for drink is not quenched. Thus in suffering he is made to pay back the wages of his error and purify his soul. Similarly, there is an independent plane of Existence called Heaven to which the virtuous are led.

APPENDIX II

Rebirth

(A Record of some Interesting Cases)

Soldier Castor, the Burmese speaker—George Castor, related some of his past experiences in the Sunday Express, London, (1935). He was a soldier born in 1889 From his boyhood he was speaking while asleep in Burmese In 1907 he joined the army In 1909 when he was 20, he was transferred to Maymyo (Burma) and there he felt that he had seen the land, lived in it, spoken the Burmese tongue, known the Irrawaddy and he told Lance Corporal Carrigon that on the other side of the Irrawaddy there was a large temple with a huge crack in the wall from top to bottom and near-by a large bell—a statement that was found true to the letter

* * *

An 18 year old boy of Jhamapukhur (Calcutta) was on his death-bed The boy's parents had thrown themselves at the feet of a Sadhu Purusha but, at the same time, had tried other means for the boy's cure. The aunt of the boy blamed the Sadhu Purusha saying that faith in the Sadhu was killing him At this the boy burst out:

"The Sadhu Purusha is not to blame You could not put your trust in him What has befallen me is nothing, when my past Karma is considered A thousand times more should I suffer In my past life, I worked in a Railway Office and murdered a person I cut him to pieces Oh ' how I pained him Where will that Karma go?

"All this happened about 50 years ago when the Suke Street Thana was in charge of a reputed officer who was known as 'Kana' sergent as he was blind in one eye He succeeded in arresting me, I escaped the gallows but got hard labour"

Then addressing his mother the boy said 'Mother, I am going now Do you know why? The person who is sleeping in the other room (referring to his father) was my son in my last birth He did all he could to make me miserable To make him feel the consequence of his past Karma I am now born as his son He must now himself feel the pain and sorrow a son can inflict on his father Karma can never be evaded and must always be endured"

(Enquiry showed that Suke Street Thana was actually in charge of an officer who was famous all over the city as the blind Sergent and who retired about 50 years ago)

Hill the South American explorer—Mr Hill writes to the Editor of the "People" "I had a strong belief that certain parts of South America were familiar to me I had a recurring dream that I was an explorer wandering alone in a tropical forest when suddenly a band of dark-skinned men appeared to whom I spoke in their tongue But for some reason, they became angry and their leaders struck me Eventually, I became a steward in the Royal Mail Liners and went to South America There. I found myself anticipating the names of obscure streets and buildings with accuracy, and I felt as I made my way about Rio de Janeiro Santos and Buenos Aires that I had surely walked there before On one voyage we took on board a Danish author at Santos One day he sent for me to come to his cabin and said

'Steward you are the victim of a remarkable coincidence or something far stranger

Then he showed me a human head taken by him from the head-hunters of Amazon reduced by a secret process to half its normal size and preserved I shuddered I know I was looking at an exact counterpart of my own face"

Bajitpur Postal Clerk s Son (Advance 15-7-36)—A three year old son of a postal clerk of Bajitpur (Faridpur) began to cry one day and insisted on going to his own home In reply to a question, he said

"I am an inhabitant of Fazilpur in Chittagong From Luxum Railway station a road leads to my village I have three sons and four daughters there. The Kalibari of Meher is not very far off from my residence It is at the Meher Kalibari that Sarvananda realized salvation There is no image of Kali There is a big banyan tree and worship is held at its root"

There is also a very tall palm tree The father of the boy had never been to Chittagong or Luxum station or to Meher Kalibari The boy sometimes sings songs which he had never heard

A Hungarian girl forgets her parents—in 1933, a 15 year old Hungarian daughter of an engineer lay on her death bed at Budapest Apparently she died, but recovered a little later, forgot her native Hungarian language completely and began to speak Spanish only She could not recognise even her parents whom she referred to as "These nice people here are very kind to me, but they are not my parents as they pretend to be" To a Spanish interpreter, she said "I am Senore Lucid Attarezde Salvio I was the wife of a working man in Madrid and had 14 children I was 40 years old and rather sick A few years ago I died, at least thought I was dying. Now I have recovered in this strange country"

She is singing Spanish songs, preparing special Spanish food and giving graphic descriptions of Madrid where she has never been

* * *

Jung Bahadur s daughter (Delhi)—Shanta, an 8 years girl of Lala Jung Bahadur, a merchant of Delhi, used to say, ever since she could talk—that in her former life she was married to a man of Mathura whose address she gave When her former husband was informed of it, he sent his brother whom the girl identified instantly Then her husband came and she recognised him at once, and told him facts which were known only to him and his former wife She also told him that she had buried one hundred rupees at a certain place in her home

* * *

Devi Prasad's child, Kanpur (Amrita Bazaar Patrika 1-5-38)—A five year old child of one Devi Prasad Bhatnagar, living in Premnagar, Kanpur, says that in his previous birth his name was Sivdayal Muktas and that he had been murdered during the Kanpur riots in 1931 when he was decoyed by two Muslim friends to a house and there murdered One day the child insisted on going to his old house where he said his former wife was lying ill He was taken there and he at once recognised his wife his children and other articles

* * *

Recites Gita at one year and a half—A correspondent from Prayagraj reports. (A B Patrika).

"A three year old boy at Jhansi can reproduce from memory the whole Srimad Bhagavad Gita and Ramayana and his pronunciation is perfect. The boy was trying in vain to speak something since he attained the age of 5 months and at the age of one year and a half he recited to his hearers Gita etc

A five year old child and Piano (People 20 6 37) —A five year old Blackpool child would rather play the piano than play with a doll She has never had a lesson, yet she plays brilliantly She can play in perfect tune any melody she hears and she adds a tune or two or her own composition

Barrister's daughter (Calcutta)—The daughter of a barrister of the Calcutta High Court, when only 3 years old, could clean the house floors excellently. On being asked she said

"I used to clean the floors in my father-in law's house in Beldanga where only myself, my father-in-law and one of his daughters lived I used to perform Puja and cook Thakurji's Bhog There was a Dole Mancha in my father-in-law's house On the Dole

Yatra Day we used to put Thakurji on a swing and smear him profusely with Avir "

The child lives in strict Achar and does not eat or sleep with her parents who are anglicised and therefore untouchables Her food is separately cooked

These facts can be easily verified even now

With strongest ties to the earth, with desires and affections hovering over earthly scenes, the generality of persons are reborn on earth immediately after death They do not sojourn in other planes of existence Some of them, as it does happen, though rarely remember their immediate past incarnation Here are two from the many cases published in the *Fate* magazine, in the year 1954

Anne, aged four said to her father 'Daddy I have been here on earth lots of times "

When he laughed Anne became indignant "I was ! I was ! I was" she cried stamping her foot Once I went to Canada as a man I remember my name even It was Lishus Faber I was a soldier and I took the gates '"

After months of research an historian found the evidence of a battle in Canada in which a single soldier had "taken the gates as Anne had said

The name of the lieutenant was Aloysius La Febre—Lishus Faber as pronounced by Anne

* * *

Vishwanath, born in Bareilly began at the age of three to give minute details of a previous life in a town called Pilibhit His parents, fearing that this meant he was going to die young, did their best to conceal their son's story

The boy named the school to which he had gone in Pilibhit in his previous existence and said the had a neighbour named Lala Sunder Lal who had a great gate, a sword and he described the parties which this wealthy man had given

To test him the boy was taken to this distant town which he had never visited before in his present life Here he correctly pointed out various parts of his original home now in ruins, including a hidden stairway Shown a group photographs, he correctly pointed out a man as his former uncle, Har Narain, and finally pointed to himself—a boy sitting amidst the group

Every detail was found to be correct His own identity was established as Laxmi Narain who had died of tuberculosis at the age of 32

Laxmi Narain's mother was still living She asked little Vishwanath numerous questions to test his memory He answered every question correctly without a moment's hesitation

Strange Case of Transmigration of a Soul

MORADABAD, August 23 —Quite a sensation has been caused following the arrival here on August 15 of a boy named Parmod from Bisauli, district Badaun, who revealed the incidents of his previous life which were found accurate to the minutest detail. Thousands of people, including several prominent figures of the city, visited him during the two days of his stay here and a clear case of transmigration of soul was established in the end

The boy, aged five and a half years, said that he was Parama Nand, brother of B Mohanlal, Proprietor of the renowned Catering Firm of Messrs Mohan Brothers, having branches in Saharanpur and Moradabad, and he died at Saharanpur on May 9, 1943, following a chronic pain in the stomach

Born at Visauli on March 15, 1944, just nine months and six days after the death of Parama Nand, as son of Babu Bankey Lal Sharma Shastri, M A, Professor in Inter College, Bisauli, the boy as early as he could pronounce the words, uttered clearly the name of Mohan, Moradabad and Saharanpur, meaning Saharanpur and later also pronounced the words Mohan Brothers Whenever he saw his relations purchasing biscuits and butter he said that he had a big biscuit factory in Moradabad. Whenever he saw some big shops in the market he said that his shop in Moradabad was bigger than any other shop He used to insist on his parents now and then to take him to Moradabad The name of the boy as entered in his Janma Kundali (horoscope) by the Pundits was also Paramanand, a strange coincidence, but the name of his elder brother being Varmod, he also began to be called as Parmod But, the child always insisted that he was Parma Nand, that he had his brothers, sons, daughter and wife at Moradabad

Mohan Lal Moves

It so happened that early this year, one Lala Raghunandan Lal of Bisauli told one of his relatives living in Moradabad about the boy and his assertions regarding his relationship with the Mohan Brothers Thereupon, the relations concerned told the whole story to Sri Mohan Lal, the proprietor of the firm Shri Mohanlal, together with some of his relatives, visited Bisauli last July and met the boy's father The boy was, however, away in some distant village with some of his relations and therefore could not be seen Shri Mohanlal requested Prof. Bankeylal to bring the boy to Moradabad and the request was succeeded It was promised that the Professor would bring the boy to Moradabad during the forthcoming Independence Day Holidays

On August 15, on alighting from the train, the boy at once recognised his brother and embraced him. On the way from the station to the residence of Shri Mohan Lal the boy recognised the Town Hall and said that his shop was now near at hand When the tonga was by-passing the shop, as arranged, in order to test the boy, he at once asked the tonga to be stopped before the shop of Mohan Brothers Then he stepped towards the house situated in front of the shop and got into the room where the late Parma Nand used to keep his articles of worship and cash box.

On entering the room he bowed in salutation. It was a very pathetic scene when he recognised his former wife and other relations and recalled several incidents of his past life which concerned them. All agreed that the incidents were true The boy could not, however, recognise his former eldest son, now 17 years, who was only 13 when Parma Nand died. When the boy recalled that all the brothers used to sit together and drink lemons etc, all the brothers and others present began to weep.

To Soda Machine

The boy then expressed his desire to go to his "gaddi" and on entering the shop went to the soda machine and explained the process of manufacturing aerated water, a thing which he had never seen in his present life He told that the water connection had been stopped, as it had really been done in order to test his memory

The boy then expressed his wish to go to Victory Hotel, owned by Sri Karam Chand, a cousin of Parma Nand He led the way to the building and to the upper storey and at once exclaimed that the rooms at present constructed on the roof were not there before

Sahu Nandlal Saran, the premier citizen of Moradabad took the boy in his car to the Meston Park, and asked him to locate the place where his civil lines branch had once been He thereupon led the company to the Gujrati Building, owned by Sahu Nandlal Saran, and pointed out the shop where once the branch of Mohan Brothers had been On his way to the Meston Park the boy recognised the Allahabad Bank, Water Works and District Jail

It may be noted that throughout his excursions to the different places in the city, done either to fulfil his wish to see places connected with his past life or to test his memory, a large number of persons were present and it was a sight worth seeing Everybody was moved The boy recognised several other places and persons who used to visit the shop during his life.

At the Public Meeting

A large public meeting was held on August 16 at the Arya Samaj where the boy's father, Prof Bankey Lal, explained the development of the boy's memory since his childhood

It was with great difficulty that the boy was taken back from Moradabad As he was not willing to go away from his old relations and the shop, he was carried away in the early hours of August 17 while asleep

A deep impression has been created upon those gentlemen here who do not believe either in God or in the transmigration of soul As a gentleman told me, "No explanation is necessary for those who believe, no explanation is possible for those who do not."

There is no need to mention that neither the boy nor his father ever visited Moradabad previously The tone, the unhesitating manner and the correctness of details narrated by him were found to be absolutely fool-proof and not even once did he falter

About twelve years ago, a similar, rather more remarkable event took place in Delhi, when Shanti Devi, aged nine years, was taken to Mathura where she identified her former husband her house and many other details connected with her previous life

—"Amrita Bazar Patrika", Aug , 1949

A Recent and Well-Known Case of Rebirth—Shanti Devi

Exactly twenty years ago, a sensational, sensational because so amazingly credible and true case of rebirth at Delhi, reported officially by a locally appointed committee consisting of enlightened, critical and competent men, was much publicised in leading Indian and foreign newspapers Born on the 12th of October, 1926, Shanti Devi, a little girl, who borne in her memory the most vivid and living pictures of the whole span of her past life beginning in the year 1902 and ending in the year 1925, began ever since she could speak, to recollect and narrate whenever the context and associations in daily life necessitated, the incidents, events and experiences in surprising detail of her past life at Muttra with her husband Pundit Kedar Nath Chaubey Her unbelieving parents not only dismissed such graphic narrations of the past life, as though they were the jabber of a child, but fervently hoped that these recollections would efface themselves from the memory of the child as she grew But, contrary to their expectation and hope, the child was insistent on recollecting more and yet more of her past life, and persisted in requesting her parents to take her to Muttra, the city of her previous birth, where she desired to show the present parents, her old house and certain things in it which only an inmate who long lived in it could have so done

At last, the child prevailed over the parents A grand uncle of the girl was called, Shanti Devi gave him the address of her husband in previous life, inquiries were made· communication was sent to her husband Pundit Kedar Nath, and surprisingly enough a response came from Pundit Kedar Nath of Muttra who in his letter, among other things, suggested to the inquiring party at Delhi to contact a relation of his, Pundit Kanji Mal, who was employed in Messrs Bhana Mal Gulzari Mal of Delhi, and give him an interview with the child, Shanti Devi No sooner Sri Kanji Mal was brought into her presence, she had not only recognised him to be the younger cousin of her husband but made most satisfactory response to the questions touching facts of an intimate nature.

Aroused to a fresh and active interest in efforts at probing into the facts of Shanti Devi's narration of the events, facts and experiences of her past life, the parents, the party and Kanji Mal called Kedar Nath Chaubey to Delhi, from Muttra When Pundit Kedar Nath Chaubey came to Delhi, with his ten-year old son, and his present wife, to see Shanti Devi, at the very first sight, Shanti Devi recognised her husband and felt greatly touched by the figure of her son, and began to shed tears After a long interchange of thought and words between Shanti Devi and her alleged husband, who was greatly moved by the veracity of the recollections and the truth of her statements, Pundit Kedar Nath confirmed the fact that this was the same Soul, viz, that of his first wife who had died at Muttra, and stated that her narration of the details in each of their particulars was true. This made the parents grant the repeated request that the girl Shanti Devi made many a time during the past few years, to go to Muttra, which the girl now reiterated with greater force as a result of the present meeting with her husband of previous life Shanti Devi not only gave out the colour of the house at Muttra, named the roads and streets leading to that house, described the Vishrant Ghat, the temple of Dwarkadhish, but stated certain things which only the former wife of Pundit Kedar Nath could alone have known She also said that she had hidden "underground" in the upper-storey room of the house at Muttra, some money, a hundred rupees from which she had vowed to give to the temple of Dwarkadhish Upon the grant of this request and wish of Shanti Devi to go to Muttra, the persuasion of the investigating committee was exerted, and the party with the committee, parents, Shanti Devi, left for Muttra As the train steamed into the Muttra Station, Shanti Devi shouted in joy "Muttra has come", "Muttra has come", and when she got down from the train, identifying in the crowd an elderly man wearing a typical Muttra dress, whom she had never met before, she came down from the arms of Deshbandhu Gupta where she was, and instinctively touched the feet of the old man stating that he was the elder brother of her husband named, Babu Ram Chaubey This fact when found to be true, was but only one among the many surprises that Shanti Devi held for the admiration and awe for her witnesses She had not only led the way to the house at Muttra, from the Railway station. but went on giving certain interesting facts as that there was on that particular road no tar earlier, and when once in the house of her description she had succeessfully passed every test that the inquiring gentleman put to her When she was taken to the Dharmashala at Muttra, she identified the "brother" of her previous birth, now in twenties, and recognised her "uncle-in-law" At every step the truth of her past narrations which were dismissed as so much of a child's jabberings were proved true, and proved true beyond doubt.

When in the house of her description, she entered its courtyard and felt dismayed at the absence of the well that was then during her previous incarnation there, noting which her husband Pundit Kedar Nath lifted up the stone covering the wall-less well and showed her the well And going upstairs, she dug up the hole where she had hidden her money, and to her uneasiness the money was not there, as it was, as Pundit Kedar Nath confessed that he had taken it from there, after the death of his former wife, now the girl Shanti Devi After this when she was taken to her "parents" house, she recognised them and both the girl and the parents sank into continued sobs, it was with great difficulty that the girl was weaned away from the parents of her previous birth, and taken to the Vishrant Ghat where she unfolded many more surprises to the investigating committee and to others by the display of the contents of the memories of her previous life Such instances as these are not uncommon in India Recently some seven years ago there was another case of another girl who has recognised her parents of her previous birth, and when a similar process of investigation had been conducted, and her narrations found true, the parents of the girl in her previous life, who are rich are now supporting her, and giving her decent education, as the present parents are poor. It is ridiculous to presume that rebirth is untrue when one has not taken pains to pursue the results of the investigations that have been conducted

Philosophy of Death

Occasionally in moments of calm contemplation, when we are thrown in an introspective mood, we sometimes wonder why God, Who is such a kind, compassionate and merciful Father, should have included death in the scheme of life The fact is, death comes as a necessity to egg us on in our evolution.

Could you just imagine of a world where there would be no death? Overpopulation even today poses as a difficult problem with all the deaths that are taking place in normal course So, imagine the extent of chaos and confusion that would result if there would be no deaths Life would no longer be worth living It would become a dull drab drudgery

Living in the same body we cannot grow beyond our bonds and ties of attachments Complete separation is necessary to make us cautious of our attachments During our brief sojourn in this world, we get so much attached to this *terra firma* that when death knocks at our door, we feel too reluctant to be torn from our family surroundings and leave our material possessions so painstakingly created Therefore to completely snap the tie of attachment, death is the only solution

Death is not only a necessity for those who die, but it is also necessary for the evolution of those who are left behind Death helps devolve responsibilities on new shoulders. They accept the challenge of life and grow in experience Father suddenly passes away Son takes up the new responsibility, bears it and enriches his treasure-house of experience When a child dies in his infancy, it may not be much of an assimilation of experience for him except for certain Karmic purgation, but it means all the more for those who are left behind. We have to grow beyond attachment, ego and desire to enjoy immunity from sufferings Thus by helping us transcend our world attachments, death plays an indispensable role

In fact, individual soul could never grow without death The evolutionary process is a long one It requires various types of experiences of poverty and riches, of purity and pollution, of ignorance and education of every country, clime, culture, race and religion It requires experiences of both the sexes as well In a single body all this is not possible to assimilate Therefore by virtue of necessity we die and are born again under different circumstances for a different set of experiences.

Assimilation of experience is also not possible without death In the post-mortem states the consciousness widens The deeds of the past lifetime have a reaction, and we learn many new lessons We often notice monkeys devouring eatables rapidly and then masticating them at leisure Similarly we masticate our experiences in a higher and wider light which shines after death. During our stay in the astral plane, the scenes of our past life flit pass our eyes one after another We begin to relieve our lives with the difference that now we are identified with all the actors in every situation We feel as we did, when we tortured some one as also like the one who was tortured by us We experience the pain of the latter This process exhausts our Karma to a degree and provides us a useful lesson. Karmic purgation occurs when both, the oppressor and also the oppressed have been able to excuse each other Retaliation only augments Karmic bondage

Death comes as a necessary drop-scene between two births It is a drop-scene in as much as the activities go on behind the curtain Thus after the assimilation of one set of experiences of one life, the individual soul is provided again with a new set of mental, emotional and Pranic body, eminently suited for his next reincarnation In this manner from life to life, he travels assimilating his diverse experiences

In normal course, the period that intervenes between two births is about four to five hundred years (in Vedantic parlance our one year is equal to one day of Pitris) But occasionally instances are there which indicate that births have been immediate Invariably in all such cases where the births have been immediate, the death has been in an accident Where we have not completed the experiences of one birth up-to-date, a second birth in similar surroundings for similar experiences, becomes absolutely necessary The other reason is that sometimes the attachments and certain resolutions are so overwhelmingly overpowering that in order to exhaust that attachment or the resolution, a second birth in the immediate future becomes absolutely necssary For illustrations we need not go to the distant past Narrations of a young girl, Mridula from Dehra Dun, who came to meet Sri Swami Sivanandaji Maharaj in 1960, corroborate the validity of my statement But it may be remembered that in all such cases the memory of the previous birth does not last long Sometimes, instances have also been found where the dead man has come back to life Sri Chandrasekhara Iyer of Hyderabad, Deccan, who resides in Sivanandashram is an example, who died and after being dead for two hours, came back to life and lives till now

At the time of death, a little distortion and contraction which we find in the body is just the efforts of the Pranic double to extricate itself from the physical body The experience is said to be painless But how does it matter even if it were painful when Death promises light behind the curtain

Mridula's Revelation of Her Last Birth

Mummy! Mummy! exclaimed a child of two years and three months, and jumped out of her mother's lap and ran towards the object of her attraction That very moment an elderly lady was getting out of a car on the road in front of Mridula's house The child ran towards the car and exclaimed incoherently, "Ah, that car is mine, and she is my mummy" The elderly lady, however ignored the child and walked past her Mridula's mother rushed out, fearing that her child might be lost on the road

But Mridula would not move from near the car, as she was looking hither and thither, as if in search of someone, her face flushed with excitement and joy Her mother, however, would share none of that, and as she felt embarassed, she took away the child forcibly back into her house That night Mridula was not her own self She went on speaking all sorts of things to her mother, like an adult recollecting the bygone days

Mridula would say. "I have and her home, mummy! We have six elephants and a car too, and there are my younger sister and daddy and so many friends Will you take me to my old mummy, please? I promised her to come Oh, how I want to go home!" And she would keep on gushing with a bable of such irrelevancies, *i e.*, as others would think of them, but not the child Her mother was thoroughly baffled, and wondered if the child was mentally all right

Days and weeks and months rolled past It was now more than six months, but Mridula would keep on harping on her old theme, her big house and car and friends. The poor mother, with all her efforts, was unable to pacify the child But the merciful Lord came to their help thus

A *Yajna* (a ritualistic rite according to Hindu tradition, when sacrificial oblations of clarified butter, etc , are poured into fire with the chanting of sacred syllables) was being performed on a large scale, in which many members of the community participated Mridula's mother, too, had gone there, taking the child with her As the ceremony came to a close, Mridula, who had been watching, ran towards two small children, of her own age, who were sitting at a distance She took off the garlands she had been wearing and put them around the necks of those children

The mother of the children, who stood nearby, was surprised, but appreciated this gesture of Mridula and said "You seem to be a very sweet child Do you know them?" Mridula at once replied "Oh I know *you* very well, though not these children," and then with bubbling emotion she asked "Don't you recognise me? I am Munnu, your elder sister Where are our daddy and mummy? How are our elephants?" And Mridula kept on speaking excitedly in this manner, many things which only an intimate member of the same family could have known

The mother of those two children was thunderstruck, and she clasped Mridula to her bosom, and asked her many questions connected with the family. She took Mridula to her mother, and told her all that had happened and asked her permission if she would allow Mridula to visit her home The mother agreed and they all drove to the young lady's house in her car

Back to the Old House

The car stopped in front of a house, and Mridula rushed out, shouting 'Oh, this is my house! Oh, here is my daddy! here is my daddy!" as she saw an elderly gentleman standing at that gate They were all baffled to see her rushing inside, and going from room to room and telling who were in each of them some years ago And then she found her room and said that here she lived, and located some books and said that these were which she had read for her M A. course She sought out her almirah and said there used to be her clothes, and also the cot where she fell ill, and lamented that she could not appear for her M A examination

Mridula asked the elderly lady of the house, with childish eagerness. "Do you know, mummy, how I felt at the time I left my body?" She pointed to her hands and feet and said. "All the nerves were taut and I felt terrible pain, and then I flew up, knowing not where, just like a bird Then I wandered here and there, and saw many luminous and joyful things Everyone was happy there Then I remembered you and I felt very sorry, for I was not with you, and then I did not remember anything" The elderly couple, who were deeply attached to their first daughter and had lost her six or seven years back, could say nothing, and as the old memories came back to them, they burst into tears

Mridula's words penetrated deep into their hearts, and they felt that the whole thing was like a dream, difficult to grasp, and yet very true, rather a revelation of profound truth, which this little unknown child unveiled before them And Mridula would not stop and insisted "I am the same Medha, whom you gave the pet name 'Munnu'. How are my friends? How is Shuklaji of D A V College? Everything here in this house is more or less the same as I had left But why have you made changes in my room? This fan does not belong here, it was in the drawing room Please speak to me, mummy! You made me promise, when I was leaving that I would come back, and here I am!" The poor lady could no longer restrain herself, and she clasped the child to her heart as tears were streaming down her cheeks

Renewal of Past Ties

Medha, who had died of tongue cancer at Dehra Dun, in her early twenties, in 1945, was doing her M A. course, but could not appear for the final examination Her deep attachment to her family had most unusually left a residue of her past memory when she was born again, to work out her Karma

She had belonged to a wealthy Vaishya (commercial) family of Dehra Dun, and she took birth in a Brahmin family (priestly caste—though nowadays few follow one's avocation according to one's own caste), in Nasik, nearly a thousand miles south, on July 31, 1949 But her Brahmin father died soon after her birth, and the mother shifted to Dehra Dun and took up a teaching career The child found the memory of her past birth in a flash, when she was two years and three months old, as stated before

Since Mridula had lived for more than twenty years in the previous birth, her attachment to her former family was naturally more deep-rooted than to her present mother, and therefore, she was more eager to stay with the former family than in her own house One can imagine the feelings of this poor lady, who had nursed her child with so much care and who loved her as her own self, having lost her husband, though Mridula's former parents, being glad to have her with them, gave her all the care she needed

The Gita says (in the second chapter, verse 22) "Just as a man casts off worn out clothes and puts on new ones so also the embodied soul casts off worn out bodies and enters new ones" This was actually proved in the case of Mridula, who was one of the very rare exceptions to have retained the memory of her past birth Perhaps it is fortunate of man in not remembering the memories of past lives, since it spares him a good deal of suffering, caused by attachment to the moorings that could hardly be regained, without discomfiture.

Immortality of Soul

Mridula had been to the Ashram of Sri Swami Sivanandaji at Rishikesh quite a few times When she had come there soon after the flash-back of her past memory, with her present mother, she was about five years old, and had a vivid recollection of her past life. She had been to Swamiji's Ashram with her both mothers, subsequently Now she is young, and her old memories have faded out a good deal, being smothered by the impressions of her childhood She is an intelligent, healthy and a perfectly normal child

Swamiji, who had listened to the child's experiences, told us that there was nothing new about them There had been similar instances in the past, but very rare and far between, as for example, the case of Shanti Devi, who, as a small child, found her former relations, more than twenty years ago These prove the immortality of the soul, which is individualized in different forms through different Samskaras or the sum total of impressions caused through actions, good or bad mental or physical Swamiji pointed out the need of freeing ourselves from the bond of Karma and to return to our original, divine source He shows us the way, by following which we can attain Godhead. He asks us to perform good actions in a spirit of detachment and dedication, and enquire "Who am I?" Swamiji's cryptic injunctions are "Be good, do good," "detach and attach" (detach the mind from the worldly objects and attach it to the Lord"). Let us all humbly pray to him to bestow upon us his grace and give us the strength to march forward and Godward.

Immediate Return After Death

Cases of Mistaken Identity

It is common to find the newspapers report of cases of persons who return to life two or three hours after death These persons are those whose identity has been mistaken by the Yama-dootas or the Messengers of the Lord of Death Two persons bearing the same name, answering to the same description, and living probably in the same village or town or city, are mistaken by the Messengers of Death, one for the other, and the wrong person is taken to the Lord of Death, only to be returned to life soon on discovery, and the right person conducted, at the same time, to the halls of Yama

Here I present the case of Sri C Reddy of Andhra Pradesh, in his own words He writes, "It is common knowledge as gathered from scriptures that after a human being casts off his mortal coil, the messengers of the Lord of Death descend down to escort the astral body of the dead person, to the Loka ordained for him in accordance with his Karmas, Prarabdha or Purushartha Those teachings of the Hindu scriptures have to be believed in before one may understand or accept the truthfulness of experience I am going to relate in my own personal case But the reader be he a believer or a non-believer in these teachings, is nevertheless going to experience sooner or later the same phenomena when his Prana, or the last breath stops to function, i e, when he dies

"I was born in an Indian princely family of South India After the advent of the Independence of India and the rule of the Congress Government, the rulers and princes of my kind became ordinary citizens of India, devoid of the previous rights, privileges and way of living, but are given only a scanty pension Having always pursued the religious life, now at the age of 73 I am a recluse and have taken shelter at the feet of my Guru Swami Sivananda Saraswati of Rishikesh, a realised Sage The truth of my experience is as follows

"In 1948, suffering from severe malaria, I became anaemic, and my doctor, a relation, gave me certain injections of insulin, which sent me into unconsciousness or coma, and forthwith I was removed to the Nursing Home nearby where I was given injection after injection to get heat into my body, but inwardly the doctor had concluded that I was dead and he had caused the news of my demise to be wired to my daughter

"What was really meant to be the death-state, I did really experience The doctor's judgment was not far wrong though he had not expected my death When I had stopped breathing physically, my astral body or soul was caught hold of by two tall black Yama-dootas who escorted me to the Yama-loka with great speed It was 11 a m and we reached our destination within 20 minutes I saw the God of Death, Yama seated on a golden pedestal *En route* I was instructed and warned by the Messengers to maintain complete silence before the Dharmaraja unless directly questioned Unto Dharmaraja I reverentially prostrated. He asked in whispers the man seated on the ground in front of Him to refer to my life-record-book, and he began to turn over pages one way and the other Their conversation I could not follow, except at the end when Dharmaraja ordered the same Yama-dootas to take me back to the mortal world, from which I concluded that I was the wrong man brought by the messengers, and perhaps somebody else answering to my name and description was destined to die at that moment"

Dead Wife Came Back as a Child

Many people have had the curious experience of visiting some place which by all available evidence they could never have seen previously but where they felt at once the conviction· "I have been here before"

Sometimes the impression is stronger so that one can say with confidence that around the next corner there will be a shop with windows containing a clearly-perceived arrangement of goods or a house with strongly individual configurations, and one is only mildly surprised when the corner is turned and the impression is confirmed

I remember, during the war, inviting an explanation of this not unusual phenomenon from a professor who had come to talk about psychology to an extremely sceptical gathering of troops The best answer he could offer was a kind of synthesis of associated ideas, for instance, that in one place you had subconsciously registered the arrangement of a picture and an ornament in another way a vase was placed on a table, in a third the gleam of brass from trophies ranged above the hearth, and that suddenly, for no very clear reason, some particular room reminded you of all these things at the same time, and established a sensation of familiarity.

The explanation was a good attempt, but so obviously unsatisfactory that I did not press one of the classic instances of "recollections" which seems to support the claims of those who believe in the ancient theory of reincarnation

It is a strange and pathetic case of a Hindu girl, about eight years old, who was being taken by her parents on a pilgrimage to Mathura, a town many miles from her birthplace to which she could not possibly have been before

On arrival, the child cried out that she recognised the town, that it was there that she had lived with her husband in her previous life, and that she must return at once to him—and to her son!

That was not all To her parents' astonishment, she led them rapidly and surely through the town to a remote street where she entered the house of the widower with one son, who, it appeared, had lost his wife about three years before this girl was born

She was so sure in her knowledge of the surrounding streets of the widower's home and his life with his past wife (as she claimed herself as such) and all the intimate details of the birth of their son and of their life together, that the man and the boy became convinced that this child of eight was indeed the reborn wife and mother

It is said that when her parents refused to allow her to stay with her "husband" and "son" as she begged, and took her back home with them she became seriously ill and raved in delirium calling incessantly for her two beloved ones that she had left behind in Mathura ! A strange story, but vouched for by several responsible Europeans in precisely these terms

* * *

For the story of the ghost with the bunch of violets, which in its way is no less unusual, I am indebted to the beautiful and talented Miss Margery Lawrence, whose own words can scarcely be improved

"I started life, as a very young girl by wanting to be an artist (says Miss Lawrence), and for sometime had a top-floor studio in a tall old house in a well-known London street The old man who owned the house had his shop on the ground floor

On the first floor directly above the shop were his offices, and the upper floors were let off, room by room, to various people, a messeuse, a maker of wax model-heads, a man who did handloom weaving, and one or two others, including myself, the proud possessor of the attic !

I had left my studio about five minutes to six one wet November night and shortly afterwards remembered something I wanted, so I ran back

As I stood waiting for a chance to cross the road, I saw the slender figure of a young girl dressed all in grey, and wearing her long fair hair streaming down her back, cross swiftly before me, somehow escaping the traffic, and vanish into the entrance of the shop

I started—surprised, at the sight of a real old-fashioned "mane" of long hair in London filled with bobbed heads, and also at the fact that as she entered the doorway of the shop she turned and seemed to smile at me, and I saw that she clutched a gigantic bunch of Parma violets Fresh violets—in November!

When I managed at last to get across the road I said to the shop assistant who was just putting up the shutters

"Who was that pretty girl with long hair and the bunch of violets who just came in and went up the stairs to Mr X's office ?"

The girl turned white, looked at me and said in a hushed voice 'Oh that miss ! did you see her? We often smell the violets, but none of us in the shop has ever seen her

It's Mr. X's only daughter She died at sixteen—years and years ago—and they say she had long fair hair below her waist, and loved violets the best of any flowers!

Sometime afterwards I found that the old man had his beloved child's body cremated, and kept the ashes in a special casket in a niche in his office, so I suppose that he thus provided a sort of 'focus' for the loving little ghost.

"That I saw her in, is certain", says Miss Lawrence, "and that I had never either heard or known of Mr X having ever had a daughter is equally certain"

As an interesting post-script to the legend of the "Abominable Snowmen" of the Himalayas, I found recently an account authenticated by Commander Rupert Gould of a series of incidents which certainly suggest the possibility that at least one of the "Mi-

Go" or "Yeti" may have wandered from its native haunts as far as southern England

In Devonshire a sensation was caused by the discovery of a series of mysterious footmarks unlike anything ever seen before It was snowy weather and the prints were clearly to be seen

The impressions were oval in shape, rather like a horse-shoe, but more pointed in the front They were made one after another in a straight line, each step about eight inches in advance of the next—and what known animal makes only a single line track of footprints one immediately after another?

The prints were seen in all sorts of peculiar places not only on the ground, but across roofs along tops of narrow walls, in gardens and enclosed courtyards as if the creature who made the prints took no account of obstacles.

In one instance, the prints marched straight up to a haystack and began again in a direct line on the further side (though there were no prints round the side of the stack or on the top) as though the creature had walked straight through the stack!

Prints were also found leading directly through dense thickets and shrubberies (the prints were clearly to be seen on the ground below the bushes) but there was no breaking of twigs or boughs as might have been expected

The prints were seen at Topsham, Lympstone, Exmouth, Teighmouth and Sawlish in South Devon in vast numbers, apparently following a definite route they vanished on the melting of the snow and have never recurred, but they have never been satisfactorily explained

Experts on animal tracks were called in, the prints (carefully drawn at the time) were analysed but no living creature has been found which makes a track in the least resembling these

—*J D Ewing.*

A Statement of Faith

I believe in God-nature as understood by Goethe, and not in any established religion The conceptions 'atheist' or 'agnostic', even the words themselves, are foreign to me I am linked to Judaism by its magnificent principles, but I am alienated from it by its unembellished severity I am linked to Evangelism by its idea of mercy, but I am removed from it by its instruction of a mediator between God and myself I am bound to India by the belief in the eternity of the world but I am separated from her by Nirvana How people can quarrel or even wage wars for the sake of religion is as incomprehensible to me as any mission in spiritual things

Propaganda is good for the masses and such subaltern institutions as the State and national economy. Just as little as we try to persuade anybody to fall in love, so we should refrain from doing so in matters of belief or metaphysics

I lift my hat before every image of God for the sake of the human beings, who are kneeling before it But I do not know a house of God to pray in; the fact that the finest of all temples, the Parthenon in Athens is without a roof signifies to me a relief for the God who was once imprisoned in it

Morality is something apart it has nothing whatsoever to do with God or religion The two greatest terrestrial gifts—beauty and health—are for me nothing but the acts of grace of some unknown power When, however, I wish to visualise my fancies, they always take the name or shape of a Greek God

I am only able to find faith in an immediate perception of the works of God without approaching Him by any system Goethe said: "Do not look for anything at the back of phenomena, they are themselves the doctrine As to the question of existence after death, I can only sum up my ideas in words, which Goethe after having expressed the thought a dozen times formulated in his old age thus "The conviction of my subsequent existence arises in me from the conception of activity, for if I work without intermission till my end, Nature is obliged to give me another form of existence when that present one is no longer able to support my mind"

I recognised God in the logical construction of a crystal no less than in that of a Bach fugue I see God in the pleading look of a dog as well as in the lovely bosom of a woman I find Him in the irridescent wings of a butterfly, and in the early morning frost which means its death He appears to me in the hairy covering of the magnolia bud, and in the hand of the child who plucks it before it can blossom. I see Him in the revolution of our times which seeks to wipe out old injustice I see Him in the smouldering eyes of a man who vows revenge upon his rival in love, and in the poised hand of the surgeon who removes a bullet from the eye after the duel I see Him in the master-hand of Leonardo, as he fixed an unearthly smile upon the lips of his divine creation, and in the caricatures which he made of men's features I see Him in a playful kitten, which seeks its playfellow in the mirror and in the murderous eyes with which it follows the movements of a robin I recognise God in the inspiration which He sends me as in a dream, and in the long labour by which I must carry it out

—*Emil Ludwig*

(The famous German Biographer)

What do Westerners Say on Death

I am, for personal purposes, convinced of the persistence of human existence beyond bodily death, and though I am unable to justify that belief in a full and complete manner, it is a belief which has been produced by scientific evidence, that is, it is based upon facts and experience, I assert emphatically that there is evidence for survival, and that some of the evidences are thoroughly good It can no more be treated superficially than any other of scientific experience

—Sir Oliver Lodge

The whole centre of gravity lies, even on the level of Psychology, in the affirmation and not in the negation of the continuity of life after death Our death is our birth to a life beyond

—W. Tudor Jones

The seeming end is not really the end for it cannot touch the true real essence of the individual.... It destroys only a semblance, a temporary representation.

—Geley

The soul must be a thing both uncreated and immortal And then it is that a human soul passes into the life of a beast, and from a beast who was once a man the soul comes back into a man again

—Plato.

"Cast into this life, as it were into an alembic, where after a previous existence which we have forgotten, we are condemned to be remade, renewed, tempered by suffering, by strife, by passion, by doubt by disease, by death All these evils we endure for our good, for our purification, and so to speak, to make us perfect From age to age, from race to race, we accomplish a tardy progress, tardy but certain, an advance of which, in spite of what all the sceptics say, the proofs are manifest If all the imperfections of our being and all the woes of our estate drive at discouraging and terrifying us, on the other hand all the more noble faculties, which have been bestowed on us that we might seek after perfection, do make for our salvation and deliver us from fear, misery and even death. Yet, a divine instinct that always grows in light and in strength helps us to comprehend that nothing in the whole world wholly dies, and that we only vanish from the things that lie about us in our earthly life, to reappear among conditions more favourable to our eternal growth in good."

—George Sand

"The doctrine of metempsychosis may almost claim to be a natural or innate belief in the human mind, if we may judge from its wide diffusion among the nations of the Earth and its prevalence throughout the historical ages"

—Professor Francis Bowen

"Although unfamiliar to Western mentality, Reincarnation is unreservedly accepted by the majority of mankind, and has been so even from the very dawn of history There are seven popular arguments in favour of Reincarnation which are more conclusive and logical than those put forward for many theological doctrines

1 That the utmost universal idea of Immortality demands it

2 That analogy makes it the most probable

3 That in many respects it harmonises with Science

4 That the nature of the Soul requires it

5 That it most completely answers the theological questions of "Original Sin" and "Future Punishment"

6 That it explains many mysterious experiences and extraordinary memories

7 That it alone solves the problem of injustice and misery which seems to dominate physical existence

The Christian teaching that "Whatsoever a man soweth that shall he also reap," is fully endorsed by the oriental teaching of Reincarnation and Karma

As there is no royal road to great attainments the presence of youthful prodigies and genius in the world is therefore a fact on the side of reincarnation Everyone has lived before through many lives and previous experiences and so everyone has different characteristics "

—Arthur E Massey

Certain Superphysical Experiences

As the daughter of a clergyman I was taken to Sunday-school two years old and to school five years old, and at the age of seven years I read the Bible and also philosophical books which I took from my father's library, and already at that time I decided to live single all my life, only interested in pondering about the mysteries of life and death In the Bible I read Paul's words "Pray unceasingly", this I did, and as an answer to my prayer, angels came to me in the night and my room was filled with light This was to me a proof of the existence of an unseen but more real world to which we were going after death

Having grown up I once experienced a physical elevation During prayer my body was lifted up in the air and held there for some moments while strong forces rushed through it, and my whole being was filled with indescribable rapture. The power was so immense that I feared to be crushed, and I had to pray for getting no more of the divine power. Then the spiritual tempest lessened, and I was gently taken to the ground Later on I had a spiritual elevation. During meditation I was lifted up in an ocean of dazzling light where nothing else was seen or heard It was as if I had no body at all but only pure existence, as if I had melted into God's aura of immense power, majesty and abundant love and bliss. Similar experiences followed, and I felt them as a kind of initiation, as my nature seemed to some degree to be changed and purified, it was as if a fragrance of the holy atmosphere in which I had merged remained with me in my daily life

Some time later I got the courage to pray for getting the same experience as Paul had, when he was lifted up in the spheres, and one night an angel, or bright spirit, came to me, lifted me out of the body and carried me out in space My first thought was that I had passed over, but the spirit told me that it was only the answer to my prayer and that I would be taken back to my body again after my visit in the spheres, which also happened I saw my body lying in my bed, and I was indeed not very glad to enter this heavy shell again. My spirit-friend came often and took me to various places in the astral world and also to higher planes But once I discovered that I was able myself to separate my astral body from my physical body and to go alone up in the spheres, and then I did so almost every night

When for the first time I came to the astral plane I was astonished to see that it appeared rather similar to our physical world, although, of course, it was of a higher vibratory nature I found that the Lord's words "In my father's house are many mansions" were literally true, as there seemed to be a mansion or habitation for every discarnated soul Some of the mansions were very modest, some rather pretty and others magnificent, according to the spiritual state of the inhabitants, and in the higher spheres I have seen mansions surpassing in magnificence any mansion on earth In the astral world there are lower and higher spheres, but everywhere the spirits enjoy a pleasant life, as there is no decay, no sickness, no decline into the vale of years, but eternal youth and beauty I have been told that no one is forced to work, but that generally the spirits are delighted to do some work, often the same as they have done on earth Painters, sculptors, musicians, composers, authors and scientists are carrying on with their work and are developing thereby, and they are joining in various societies according to mutual interests, just as on earth There are learning institutions for science, art and music, and many are working there as teachers; I have visited some universities and have attended highly interesting lectures The different religions are also represented and have their churches and lodges, and our Lord is worshipped there just as on earth and nobody can doubt His existence, as He often speaks to the various groups His presence alone is a blessing to all So his words to the disciples· "Where I am there ye may be also", is a wonderful reality

Generally the spirits are using their own language, but there is a universal language which all educated spirits understand, and which everybody has an opportunity to learn

Perhaps I should not omit to mention that every discarnated soul, when entering the astral world, has to go through a period of retrospection and introspection that corresponds to our idea of the purgatory, as all his deeds, both his good and bad actions and his good and bad words have been recorded by invisible supervisors who have followed him during all his life on earth So it has come true that "men shall give account of every idle word that they have spoken, and that by their words they shall be justified, and by their words they shall be condemned", and our Lord's words "There is nothing concealed that shall not be revealed, and nothing hid that shall not be made known Therefore whatsoever ye have spoken in darkness shall be heard in the light, and what ye have spoken into the ear in the inner chambers shall be proclaimed upon the housetops", are indeed a reality For many it is an agony to go through these records and be confronted with their own bad actions and words, but for others it is rather a joy to see the fruits of their idealistic endeavours

In the higher spheres I have met many highly developed spirits, and some of them told me that we had lived together in what they call "the great incarnation", when our Lord wandered on earth I did not remember that incarnation, whereas I have had various visions from other incarnations, some of them great, some rather common, and I might mention that it was an astonishing experience, when for the first time I found myself in a man's body, but then I understood why I had always felt my own being more as a man than as a woman

On looking back into my earlier incarnations it became evident to me that our present being, in reality, is but a fragment of our real being, and that our consciousness is but a part of our total consciousness, which will not appear until we have gone through the sum of all incarnations In each incarnation we have to develop certain qualities and to serve in special environments, and therefore it has been necessary to shut off the memory of earlier incarnations, as this would only be a burden to us In each incarnation we are also given a new opportunity to choose between the difficult way that leads unto life and the broad way that leads to perdition

By the so-called "second-sight" I have seen the most important events in my life, before they happened in reality I shall only state one example Before I had got my B A degree at the university of Copenhagen I once, during meditation, suddenly found myself sitting in a lecture room at the university, giving a lecture to a large audience When the vision had faded away, I thought that it might signify that some day I would be sitting in that lecture room as a professor Unfortunately this interpretation was wrong, but still the vision came true, as some time later my professor invited me to give a series of lectures on medieval mysticism which took place in just the same lecture room that I had seen in my vision

Once I decided to try if I should be able, by an act of will, to break through the barrier of time and space, and to project my consciousness back into the past and also out into the future, to a certain place and time, and to watch the events that had once taken place, respectively were going to take place there. These experiments proved successful, and in every case I got a verification

I have examined the nature of the astral body and its relation to the physical body, and I have found that our consciousness is by no means dependent on the physical brain, whereas our physical body is throughout dependent on the astral body It simply cannot move a single muscle, when the astral body is withdrawn

In my astral body I have been walking in the streets of Copenhagen, trying in vain to influence people, and I have visited places where I had not been before, in order to get a verification, when later I went there in my physical body In every case I got a verification, and twice I have been seen by persons who were present and who afterwards told me about my peculiar appearance As I was able to tell them what they had been doing during my astral visit, they were obliged to believe that I had really been present.

I might also mention that I have once, together with a spirit-friend, visited a subterraneal city It was indeed a peculiar experience to go downwards into the earth and find a bright and beautiful city My spirit-friend took me to a great temple in Greek style with columns of marble, where I met the leader of the city who told me about the work which took place there

Once I discovered that I was able, through intense concentration, to dematerialize and rematerialize physical matter, and of course it was both astonishing and interesting, I have, however, made no further experiments in that direction, as I am more interested in taking time to meditate on the mysterious regions in the inner world, whose sublime and glorious beauty and fineness cannot be described, as our language has no words to cover those extraordinary experiences

I have often been asked about my Sadhanas, and first of all I might mention, that I have found that, more than any exercise, it is the burning desire that opens the door for the influx from on high

It is the complete surrender, the opening of mind and soul to the eternal spirit, that opens the centres I have heard about aspirants who cannot understand why they have had no results, although they have practised Yoga-exercises during a long period of years, and I feel convinced that it is the fervent yearning for union with the supreme Spirit that is lacking It is, however, of great importance to pray or meditate before going to sleep, and thereby to cleanse the mind from earthly thoughts, before entering the subconscious state during sleep I always try both to deepen and to expand my consciousness before sleeping, in order to get in connection with the Great within, which is always in close touch with the heavenly spheres I dare say, that the deepening of the consciousness before sleeping is one of the most important exercises I also meditate in the morning and thereby get the necessary strength for my daily work, and when resting during the day I try to place my consciousness in touch with the divine spirit and to forget my personal self. When feeling the higher power mysteriously moving in the depths of our mind, we should not be afraid but keep quiet and thoroughly receptive then we are anointed by the spirit

—*K.M , Copenhagen (Denmark).*

GLOSSARY

ACHARA Right conduct.

ACHARYAS Teachers, preceptors

ADHARMA Averse to religion, Unrighteousness

ADITYA Sun

AGNI. Fire

AHAMKARA Egoism, pride

AMANAVA PURUSHA Superman

APANA A kind of breath circulating in the human body, the down-going breath

APSARAS Dancers in Heaven—girl dancers

APURVA Extraordinary, the hidden power or force of a Karma which brings its fruits in the future

ARYA SAMAJ A religious society which converts Muslims to Hindu religion

ASANA Posture

ASHRAMAS· Hermitages; orders of life

ATMA, ATMAN Soul.

ATMA PURANA A sacred book of self-knowledge

AVIDYA Ignorance

AVIR Red smear

AYURVEDA Indian system of medicine.

BAUDDHAS Followers of the Buddha.

BHAGAVATA, BHAGAVATAM A sacred book of Hindus

BHAKTAS Devotees

BHAKTI· Devotion.

BHARATA Son of king Dushyanta

BHASHYA Translation, commentary

BHAV, BHAVA Feeling

BHAYANAKA SHABDA Horrible sound

BHOGA Enjoyment

BRAHMA, BRAHMAN Supreme Lord

BRAHMA JNANA Knowledge of the Supreme Lord

BRAHMA SUTRAS Fundamental principles of religion a sacred book

BRAHMA VIDYA Knowledge of Brahman

BRAHMACHARYA Celibacy

BRAHMIN The highest of the four Hindu castes

BUDDHI Intellect

BUNDEHESH A name of a book

CHAITANYA Consciousness

CHAKRAS Spiritual centres in astral tubes

CHANDALA The meanest person

CHHANDOGYA UPANISHAD A sacred book

CHANDRALOKA One of the planes of Heaven.

CHIT, CHITTA Consciousness

CHITRAGUPTA Name of a king

CHITRAKETU Name of an artist

DAIVIC Concerning Gods

DAMA Control of the senses

DEVARCHANA Worship of gods

DEVAYANA Path which leads to the gods

DHARANA Faith, belief concentration of mind

DHARMA RAJA The God who decides the fate of souls after death.

DHARMASHALA Free rest-house

DHRITARASHTRA Blind father of Kauravas—a ruling prince

DHYANA Meditation.

DIGAMBARA JAINS A Jain religious sect in India

DOLA MANCHA Swinging bed

DOLA YATRA Procession of the God in the swing

DOSHAS Faults, impurities

DRISHTI Sight

DHRUVA Name of a boy ascetic

DURGA Consort of Lord Siva

GAYATRI JAPA Repetition of Gayatri hymn

GITA. A sacred book, a universal Gospel

GOPIS Playmates of Lord Krishna (female)

GRIHASTHA Married period of one's life

GUNAS Virtues

GURU Spiritual preceptor

GURU GRANTH SAHIB Holy book of the Sikhs

GURU MANTRA Mantra in which one has been initiated by the Guru

GURU NANAK A holy sage who founded the Sikh religion

HARI Name of God

HATHA YOGA A kind of Yoga

ICHHA MRITYU Dying at will

INDRA King of Heavenly people

INDRIYAS Senses

ISHWARA God

JAINS A religious body in India

JAPA Repetition of Mantras (Hymns)

JIVA Soul

JNANA INDRIYAS Astral tubes pertaining to knowledge in a human body—Five senses

JNANA· Knowledge

JNANI Wise man

JNANESHWARI A book written by Saint Jnaneshwar

KAIVALYA Final Spiritual Beatitude

KALALA First stage in evolution of human body in the womb

KAMA Passion, desire

KARMA Action, deed

KARMA KANDA A chapter on human actions and practices

KARMASTHANA A place of action

KATHAS Recitation of holy scriptures

KATHOPANISHAD A sacred book

KAUNTEYA Arjuna—a warrior and devotee of Lord Krishna

KIRTAN Recitation of holy hymns

KRISHNA Name of God

KSHATRIYA Second of the Hindu castes

KUBERA. God of Wealth

KUMBHIPAKA One of the Hells

KUNDALINI SAKTI The inner spiritual power in the human body

KURUS A warrior clan who fought in the famous Mahabharata war

LINGA SARIRA (SAREERA) The subtle body

LOKAYATIKAS A name of a clan

MADULI Like a bracelet

MAHA MRITYUNJAYA MANTRA A hymn dedicated to Lord Siva with a view to overpower death

MAHABHARATA The great epic of Hindus

MANES One of the heavenly beings, Pitris or forefathers

MANTRAS Hymns

MANUSMRITI A sacred book—Hindu Code of Law

MAYA Illusive power, veiling power

MOHA Attachment

MOKSHA Liberation, ultimate release from the cycle of birth and death

MOTHER KALI Name of a Goddess of destruction

MOUNA Silence

MUKTAS Emancipated souls

MUKTI Emancipation.

MUTTER MALA A bracelet which is worn by ladies

NADIS Astral tubes, nerves

NAMA SMARANA Repetition of name of God

NARADA Name of an ascetic mentioned in Hindu Scriptures

NARAYANA Name of God.

NARADEEYA PURANA A sacred book

NIRVANA Emancipation, Moksha

NIRVIKALPA Without the modifications of the mind

NIYAMA Religious rules—second step in Raja Yoga

OM Name of Supreme Lord

PADODAKA Water in which feet of a Deity have been washed

PANCHAGNI VIDYA Knowledge relating to fires, described in the Upanishads

PANDITS, PUNDITS Learned persons

PARIJATA A name of a tree.

PARIKSHIT A name of a king

PARAMATMA Supreme Self

PARISHISHTA Appendix to a book

PARTHA Name of Arjuna

PASCHIMOTTANASANA A name of a posture in Yoga

PATANJALI MAHARSHI A name of a sage

PINDA Offering of rice which a son does for the departed soul of his ancestors

PITRIS Ancestors

PRAJAPATI Name of God—creator of this Universe

PRAKRITI Nature

PRANA Vital energy

PRANAYAMA Regulation of breath

PRANAYAMA Science of breathing

PRASNOTTARI Questions and answers

PREMA Divine love

PRITHVI Earth plane

PUJA Worship

PURANAS Name of Hindu sacred books

PURUSHA Man

RAJA BHARATA Name of a king

RAJA YOGA A form of Yoga

RAJA YOGIC SAMYAMA Perfect restraint stated in Raja Yoga

RAJAS Passion

RAKSHASAS Wicked people

RAMAYANA A name of an epic

RAURAVA One of the stages in Hell.

RISHIS Sages, seers of the secrets of life

RUDRA God of destruction—another name of Lord Siva

SADHAKA Spiritual practitioner

SADHANA Spiritual practice

SADHU A good person

SAKTI Power

SAMA Equal, balanced state of mind

SAMADHI Superconscious state

SAMSARA The process of worldly life

SAMSKARAS Impressions

SAMYAMA Restraint

SANDHYA Worship—(evening time)

SANKARA Name of God

SANKARACHARYA A Hindu holy sage

SANKHYA A school of philosophy

SANNYASA Stage of life when a person is supposed to renounce the world

SANNYASI One who has embraced the life of complete renunciation

SAPINDA One who deserves Pinda-Dana

SARVAVIDYA All-pervading knowledge

SAT-CHIT-ANANDA SWAROOPA God who is Truth, Consciousness and Bliss

SATSANGA Spiritual assembly

SATTWA Purity

SHRADDHA, SRADDHA. A ceremony which the eldest son must perform after the death of his father

SHUDRA Fourth of the Hindu castes (lowest)

SIDDHA Perfected and devoted to Yoga

SIRSHASANA A posture in Yoga

SISUPALA Name of a wicked king

SLOKAS Hymns

SMRITI Holy scriptures

SRIMAD BHAGAVATA A holy book of Hindus

SRUTI Holy scriptures

SURYALOKA One of the planes in Heaven

SUTRADHARA A person who introduces actors in the opening of a show

SWAMIS Learned persons who have renounced the world

TAKSHAKA. One kind of snake

TAMAS Darkness

TAPAS Penance

TARPANA Offering

TATTWA Element

TEJAS· Aura

TAIJASA A person with aura

THAKURJI God

THANA A police station

TIRTHAS Holy places

TITTIRIS Butterflies

TONGA A horse-carriage

TULASI A holy plant

UDANA VAYU One of the five vital airs, functioning in the throat

UPANISHADS Dialogues of spiritual wisdom between Rishis or seers and Brahmachari-students, i e, the seekers who sought spiritual instruction, on the basis of strict control of sex-desire and reverence for the teachers or Gurus

VAIKUNTHA Abode of God

VAIRAGYA Renunciation

VAISESHIKAS One of the religious sects of India

VAISHYA Third of the Hindu castes

VAITARANI A stage in Hell

VANAPRASTHA A period of life which begins after one has finished the household period of life i e, after 50 years of age and up to 75 years of age

VAHNI Fire

VARUNA God of water

VASANAS Impressions of actions that remain in the mankind

VASUDEVA Name of God

VEDANTA Philosophy

VEDANTINS Those who study and practise spiritual philosophy

VEDAS Holy books of Hindus

VICHARAS. Thoughts

VIDEHAMUKTI Emancipation

VIDYA Knowledge, learning

VIMANAS Carriers which fly in the air—like modern aeroplanes

VIROCHANA Name of a philosopher

VISHNU One of the names of God

VISWANATHA Name of God.

VIVEKA Awakening, Discrimination

VYANA One of the five vital airs, that pervades the whole body

YAJUR VEDA Holy book of Hindus

YAKSHA One of the heavenly bodies

YAMA God of Death

YOGA Superconscious state, union with God

YOGA SADHANA Practice of Yoga

YOGI One who practises Yoga

YOJANAS Schemes

YONIS Different forms of life in the universe

YUDHISHTHIRA Name of a king who fought in Mahabharata war

NOTE —*Chapter VI deals with various planes of the Heaven including Supra-physical planes Most of the names appearing in this chapter relate to various names of Gods, their attendants—male and female—mountains, rivers, trees, etc, so definition of such words has been omitted from glossary*

THE DIVINE LIFE SOCIETY

The Divine Life Society was founded by His Holiness Sri Swami Sivanandaji Maharaj in 1936 for the widest possible propagation of the most precious and the best elements of the great culture and living Idealism of Inner India His Holiness was striving ceaselessly through this Society and the Ashram to bring aboout a world-wide dissemination of the vital, ethical and spiritual idealism of India and to propagate, broadcast the knowledge of Yoga, Vedanta, Dharma and the ideal life of divine virtues, right conduct, selfless service, universal brotherhood and the unity of life as a whole

The Headquarters of this Society are housed at Sivanandanagar, on the banks of the Ganges at Rishikesh, at the foothills of the Himalayas Here labours a band of Sannyasins, whose lives are entirely dedicated to the service of humanity, to learn and put into practice the Yoga of Synthesis and to function actively as dynamic centres of spirituality. The Society has as its aim the awakening of all humanity to the true and lofty purpose of life, enlightening them on the various means and methods of attaining the Goal, and inspiring them and urging them to strive for its attainment

The Divine Life Society carries out its object of a world-wide revival of spirituality through publication of books, pamphlets and magazines dealing scientifically with all the aspects of Yoga and Vedanta, religion, philosophy and ancient medicine, holding and arranging religious conferences and discourses, establishing training centres for the practice of Yoga and the revival of culture, and taking such other steps from time to time as may be necessary for bringing about a quick, moral and spiritual regeneration in the world.

This Ashram serves as a place of preservation of the ancient tradition and cultural practices that have come down as a time-honoured heritage. It has been built up to serve as a model of many-sided, altruistic activity, an ideal to copy, intended to bring about a complete unfoldment of the human personality, and to reveal the essential blending together of all sides of human nature. The Ashram also functions as an ideal place of retreat for the educated citizen of the world, wherein he can renew himself and recreate and refresh his being physically, mentally, morally and spiritually

An allopathic General Hospital attached to the Society, with arrangements for indoor patients, does valuable service in making available free medical and surgical aid to the suffering Additional departments have been added thereto in diathermy and X-ray The reputed Ayurvedic Pharmaceutical Works prepares genuine and high-quality Ayurvedic medicines that have gained a name in India and abroad. A well-equipped Eye-Hospital does immense service to the patients of the neighbourhood and provides them with indoor treatment In-patients of these two Hospitals are given food and medicines free of cost The Annakshetra (common kitchen) is open to the poor and the needy and any pilgrim requiring such assistance A well-fitted Photo Studio equipped on modern lines has prepared valuable movie films of the different Yoga exercises and Yoga processes A beautiful Temple and prayer hall provide scope for devotional exercises and prayer in an ideal setting Regular worship is conducted daily for the weal of humanity A Yoga-museum serves to give in brief and at a glance the essence of Yoga and Vedanta. The Society runs a "Yoga-Vedanta Forest Academy" which trains students from all parts of India as well as from other countries like Europe, America, Africa, Indonesia and Malaya The Academy is established to impart specialised knowledge of the different techniques of Yoga and to prepare the students for the higher meditation on the spiritual path as also to train them in the unselfish service of humanity based on the spirit of universal love and brotherhood

The maintenance of perfect health is regarded as essential for undertaking spiritual Sadhana, and for that purpose classes in Yogic Physical Training are regularly conducted. For the purpose of Spiritual Sadhana, courses and lectures are regularly conducted in the Ashram premises. The Ashram also affords individual instructions in practical Sadhana. Apart from the inmates, members of the public in India and from abroad visit the Ashram in large numbers to study and practise Yoga and philosophy and are also afforded free facilities for boarding and lodging at the Ashram

The main objects of this Society, therefore, comprehend the spread of education, philosophy and spiritual knowledge without reference to caste or creed, so as to embrace all religions in general, relief of the poor through the Annakshetra, and medical relief The Yoga-Vedanta Forest Academy Press, run by this charitable Institution, does the work of publication of books and periodicals for making spiritual and cultural knowledge available Special publications on the prevention and cure of diseases and on maintaining health have been and are being released by the Society through this Press

Membership of the Divine Life Society is open to all those who pledge themselves to practise Ahimsa, Satya and Brahmacharya (to the best of their ability) and who pay an admission fee of Rs 5 00 and an annual subscription of Rs 2.50 P The members are entitled to the free literature published by the Society, as also a *Sadhana Set*, containing the preliminary lessons on Sadhana

The Correspondence Section clears the doubts and difficulties of aspirants in their spiritual Sadhana. Individual replies sent from the Institution provide illuminating guidance, hope and courage to the faltering and the despondent. A unique method of maintaining spiritual evolution is to induce constant introspection and to bring about a quick progress in Sadhana.

The Free Literature department regularly distributes a number of pamphlets, leaflets and messages to provide spiritual enlightenment and consolation to the aspirants

For the spread of education and knowledge, the Society undertakes the publication of books, pamphlets and magazines dealing with Philosophy, Religion and Medicine, the bulk of which is distributed free to libraries, universities and individual aspirants. The Society also brings out the Journals, "The Divine Life" (monthly), "Health and Long Life" (monthly) 'Wisdom Light" (monthly), "Branch Gazette" (monthly), and "Yoga-Vedanta" (Hindi monthly)

The Divine Life Society does not restrict its benefits to members of any particular community or faith The objective kept in mind is the expounding of the truth underlying the tenets of every religion on a universal basis Thus the WORLD PARLIAMENT OF RELIGIONS was held in April, 1953, and in 1957 a Commemoration Volume relating to all religions was published This Volume was supplied free to all public libraries and university libraries in India and abroad Pamphlets on Islam, Christianity and Buddhism, etc, have been brought out from time to time Under guidance from the Headquarters of the Divine Life Society, aspirants are locally conducting schools of Yoga in different parts of the world e g. Copenhagen (Denmark), Hamburg (Germany), London (England), Melbourne (Australia), Montreal (Canada), Illinois (U S.A.), Durban (South Africa), Kuala Lumpur (Malaysia), etc.

The fundamental aims and objects of the Divine Life Society as a whole, are purely spiritual, entirely non-sectarian, universally applicable and perfectly tolerant. The society offers a peaceful haven wherein is provided ample opportunity and actual help for the restoration of peace to the troubled, conflict-ridden and psychologically traumatised personality of the modern man. The aim is Life in the Universal Divine.